D0090213

Learning To Be Capitalists

Learning To Be Capitalists

Entrepreneurs in Vietnam's Transition Economy

Annette Miae Kim

OXFORD

UNIVERSITY PRESS

2008

OXFORD
UNIVERSITY PRESS

Oxford University Press, Inc., publishes works that further
Oxford University's objective of excellence
in research, scholarship, and education

Oxford   New York
Auckland   Cape Town   Dar es Salaam   Hong Kong   Karachi
Kuala Lumpur   Madrid   Melbourne   Mexico City   Nairobi
New Delhi   Shanghai   Taipei   Toronto

With offices in
Argentina   Austria   Brazil   Chile   Czech Republic   France   Greece
Guatemala   Hungary   Italy   Japan   Poland   Portugal   Singapore
South Korea   Switzerland   Thailand   Turkey   Ukraine   Vietnam

Published by Oxford University Press, Inc.
198 Madison Avenue, New York, New York 10016

www.oup.com

Oxford is a registered trademark of Oxford University Press

Library of Congress Cataloging-in-Publication Data
Kim, Annette Miae.
Learning to be capitalists : entrepreneurs in Vietnam's
transition economy / Annette Miae Kim.
p. cm.
Includes bibliographical references and index.
ISBN 978-0-19-536939-7
1. Capitalism—Vietnam.   2. Entrepreneurship—Vietnam.
3. Vietnam—Economic policy.   I. Title.
HC444.K54 2008
338'.0409597—dc22   2007047159

2 4 6 8 9 7 5 3 1

Printed in the United States of America
on acid-free paper

To my mother and father
and
Roland and Joshua

Acknowledgments

This book was more than a decade in the making, and many people and institutions helped the research project evolve along the way. My father is the one who first suggested to me that I focus on the Asian transition countries, as a roundabout way to approach my interest in understanding North Korea and its possible future. But it was the advisor of my doctoral studies at Berkeley, David Dowall, who first brought me to Ho Chi Minh City as one of his research assistants, cementing my future engagement with Vietnam. He also later astutely advised me that rather than collecting statistics, I had a historic opportunity to directly interact with the first generation of real estate developers in Vietnam.

During my fieldwork, innumerable people helped me with a level of gentleness and generosity that graduate students rarely see. They really are too many to mention, but I have to at least profusely thank dear friends Hanh Bui, Le Tuyen, Le Thi Thanh Loan, Le Nguyen Huong Giang, and Nga. They shared their lives with me, allowed me to enter their social networks, and corralled others to help me. I am also grateful to Ton Gia Huyen, Gosta Palmkvist, Iris Ting, Khoi Vo Dac, Thuy Hang Thi To, Kazimierz Kirejczyk, and Joe Tham for providing key introductions and generous assistance.

Throughout the years, many institutions provided funding that enabled me to return to Vietnam several times and to pursue new lines of inquiry. The Fulbright Commission's support allowed me to live in Ho Chi Minh City for a year. Other financial support came through the University of California. The Lincoln Institute of Land Policy and the World Bank provided grants to collect data. Funds from the Massachusetts Institute of Technology and the William Davidson Institute allowed me to pursue comparative research in other transition countries and afforded me the time to write.

The writing process and the development of my ideas benefited from the engagement and critical feedback of several colleagues: Alice Amsden, Diane Davis, Karen Polenske, Bish Sanyal, Lawrence Susskind, Judith Tendler, Phil Thompson, and Lawrence Vale. I greatly appreciated the interest in and comments on my research from Dale Goldhaber, Mark Granovetter, Youtien Hsing, Yasheng Huang, Katharina Pistor, Gérard Roland, Susan Silbey, Christopher Woodruff, and Ezra Zuckerman.

I am also thankful for my friends' optimism and confidence in what I was doing, especially when mine wavered: Sarah, Hubert, Kimberly, Jeanette, Michele, Lan-chih, Laura, Jan, Elizabeth, Nancy, Julie, and Mrs. Min. I am also grateful for excellent research assistance from Kathy Hoag, Yu Li, Li Li, Claudine Stuchell, Georgeta Vidican, and my brother David Kim.

And, last but not least, I would like to thank Roland and my joy Joshua for their patience, flexibility, and good cheer as I holed up writing. Your smiles and hugs were a relief to come home to during all of this.

Contents

Learning To Be Capitalists

1

Introduction

Vietnam's Transition and the Emergence of Entrepreneurs

In the autumn of 2000, I went to Saigon to find real estate developers. I wondered where this first generation of entrepreneurs had come from, given that only eight years earlier they would have been considered criminals. Private land developers epitomize capitalism, and their activities are particularly difficult for a Communist government to legitimate: windfall profiting from state-owned land. But from my previous visits I knew that there were now large, private land development projects sprouting everywhere in the city. Vietnam seemed to be defying many experts who ranked it as one of the worst places to conduct business.

I was not sure how I was going to find them, though, because there were no reliable listings of private land development companies. I got off the plane with flimsy contacts and doubts about whether I would be able to get any answers. I had been to Vietnam twice before and knew it was a challenging research environment. On my first trip in 1996, a fellow research assistant was detained by the police for missing one of the layers of government approval required to even talk to people while we were doing household surveys. But during those trips I realized at least two things. One was that a sense of personal empathy between me and those interviewed could unleash a wealth of information. After I had gotten through my short list of prescribed questions, some households had wanted me to stay longer to eat and talk with them. They had more that they wanted to share with me than could be contained in a survey. I also realized that I should avoid official government channels as much as possible.

Worried about not being able to gain access to any information, I had developed contingency plans for my contingency plans. But despite my low expectations, through polite persistence and some luck I was able to collect many kinds of data during that year. I conducted market price surveys, obtained government statistics and maps, and even commissioned satellite photos of the city to record the new urban growth patterns. Some of the data is included in this book, but in the end things like the snapshots taken from space were probably the least substantively interesting, although technologically dazzling. There was something happening on a day-to-day basis, the new ways people were relating and transacting with one another, that was the most fascinating phenomenon.

The rapid changes were particularly amazing to me after having attempted development work in places like Nairobi, Kenya, during the 1990s. Showing up to work at my pan-African housing organization was a depressing ritual in futility as the infrastructure around us steadily deteriorated. By contrast, I woke up each morning in Ho Chi Minh City (HCMC)[1] to the sounds of construction and commerce—new sidewalks, cafés, shops. Most foreign academics I knew preferred to live in Hanoi, with its elegant French town planning, artistic community, and orderliness. But to me HCMC, with its crassness and hustling, was the more interesting city. There was a sense of palpable energy and laid-back experimentation suspended in the heat and humidity. People could and did test boundaries, form new relationships, start new ventures.

It was also a time when locals were still curious about foreigners and wanted to befriend them. When I deplaned I had one acquaintance expecting me, a former Harvard teaching assistant who was now part of a Fulbright program training Vietnamese civil servants. Within a week, that contact led me to meet more and more people. Despite being someone who is squeamish about networking, I found that these contacts mushroomed almost effortlessly in HCMC, and because I eventually lived unregistered with a local household, I was not under government scrutiny. I was introduced to people through links of friendship. In marked contrast to Hanoi, here people spoke with amazing candor about their activities and perspectives.

Soon I was immersed in the world of Vietnamese real estate as seen from the point of view of the developers and others working in the newly formed industry. They walked with me around their projects, introduced me to their associates, shared documents and maps. They also sat for hours, usually over meals or drinks, explaining what they do, how they do it, and how their world works.

Living in HCMC also allowed me to view the developers within the context of their changing society. For example, it was telling to see what they did not mention in relation to the social upheaval taking place around their urban development projects. It was also amusing to see that certain reforms that were supposed to be important to them, such as legislation securing their property rights, had little impact on their activities.

These experiences gave me insight into one of the most sought-after goals of international development: the emergence of entrepreneurs and private firms that promote investment and enlarge the economy. In roughly fifteen years, Vietnam has transitioned from being one of the poorest developing countries to the second fastest growing country in the world. Success cases are rare in international development, especially ones that happen so quickly. Even more beguiling, Vietnam did not follow the economic reforms espoused by the major development institutions. Organizations such as the IMF and the World Bank have been trying for decades to design reform policies that will unleash a market economy in developing and transition countries. Their reform strategies assume that people are entrepreneurs at heart but are prevented by their governments and a lack of technology, financing, or infrastructure from acting as their natural entrepreneurial selves. Yet entrepreneurs and private firms seemed to have emerged in Vietnam despite these constraints.

This book is an account of the remarkably rapid changes I have seen in Vietnam and in Vietnamese people during the 1990s and 2000s. The unusual opportunity I had to engage with some of the first generation of entrepreneurs and the amazingly rich time I spent in the country prompted me to write this book in order to discuss several things that I believe have been missing or underdeveloped in mainstream international development discourse.

The Mystery of Vietnamese Capitalism and the Puzzle of Transition

The international business and development community is currently intrigued by Vietnam because of its rapid growth and potential. "There's probably no other country in the world that, over the last 15 years, has moved its development so far and so fast," according to Klaus Rohland, the World Bank's Vietnam country director from 2002 to 2007. Real income has grown 7.3 percent a year over the past ten years. Poverty levels have dropped from about 60 percent to less than 20 percent. World Bank President Robert Zoellick, who visited Vietnam in one of his first tours in office, has said that "Vietnam has the potential to be one of the great success stories in development" (World Bank 2007).

It is quite a turnaround in opinion from the days when Vietnam was mostly mentioned in policy circles for having some of the most inappropriate reforms among the transition economies (IMF 2000; Heritage Foundation 2004). As many

Communist countries started to make the transition to a market economy during the late 1980s, typical reform strategies revolved around the free market paradigm that is still being espoused, particularly for developing countries. These reforms, sometimes referred to as the Washington Consensus, advocate decreasing the state's presence in the economy through privatizing state-owned property, decentralizing power to lower levels of government, and deregulating state oversight of the economy, while emphasizing the establishment of the legal and private financial institutions that Western industrialized countries have. The rationale is that once the government stays out of the way, laws and financing will provide adequate incentives for people, especially foreign firms, to make investments and be entrepreneurial, and therefore market capitalism should emerge naturally.

However, after more than two decades of transition, it is apparent that there is great diversity in how well economies have been growing and the shape their markets have taken (Roland 2000). A study published by the International Monetary Fund examined the progress of transition and found great differences in GDP growth rates (IMF 2000). It suggested the variation in economic outcomes was the result of variation in financing and legal institutions. The authors developed an indicator of "institutional quality" and ranked transition countries according to its criteria. Ironically, in their own tables they show China and Vietnam as having some of the lowest institutional quality but the fastest economic growth.

Figure 1.1 is a heuristic diagram that shows that the Washington Consensus model does not account for the diversity of empirical outcomes. Separated into two rows are those that followed the conventional free market reforms that preoccupy mainstream development policy discourse and those that did not. The columns show that some countries have grown tremendously while others have either been stagnant or disenchantingly slow in their rate of change.

The reform strategies do not necessarily correlate with economic outcomes. There were some who followed the reforms

Transition Reforms	Economic growth, private firm formation, entrepreneurialism	
	+	−
Conventional	A poster child	B step-child
Unconventional	C challengers	D scapegoats

Figure 1.1 The puzzle of transition.

but did not fare well, category B. Often these countries have been blamed for not following the conventional reforms closely enough because they lacked the "political will" to carry them out fully. But like Tolstoy's unhappy families, each country has its own reasons for its economic troubles. These factors are outside the scope of this book, but have been well discussed in the literature.

Most of the international development policy literature has focused on comparing cases in categories A and D, which only serves to reify that conventional reforms work and unconventional ones do not. For example, Douglass North (2005) compares the rise of the West with the Soviet Union's failure rather than asking why other Communist countries such as China and Vietnam have succeeded. Hernando de Soto (2000) goes as far as to streamline the conventional reforms down to one magic bullet: property title registration. He argues that unlike in most developing countries, in the West property rights are so secure that they can be used as collateral for financing, thereby unleashing "dead" capital. While his theory is wildly popular with politicians, particularly in Latin America, scholars have questioned his interpretation of the history of financial institutions and the appropriateness of making comparisons between developing countries and the United States or western Europe and for not

addressing the political and ethical implications of his sugges-
tions (Woodruff 2001; Krueckeberg 2004). Moreover, decades of
property title regularization projects in many countries around
the world have not demonstrated any systemic effect.

These points aside, in his *Mystery of Capital* de Soto is quiet
about the two fastest growing countries in the world, China and
Vietnam, neither of which has the kind of private property rights
institutions he proposes. They also have not had major changes
in political regimes, have not established the rule of law or disciplined finance institutions, and in both countries the state still
intervenes heavily in the economy. The bigger question to rock
the conventional paradigm is not why the typical reform pack-
ages have not worked in so many places, but why places like
Vietnam and China have grown market economies so rapidly.
These cases remain mysteries. Analytically, it is more logical to
focus on learning from successes, especially those that seem to
challenge our current theories. What happened in category A
and C countries?

One argument is that category C countries do not have
"real" capitalism. Rather, some claim that the rapid growth in
the Asian transition is merely the result of industrialization,
since these countries started transition at a lower level of development than their European counterparts. I think few now
would argue that Vietnam and China are not integrated into
the global economy. But in any case, given their initial conditions, the question is only more compelling: how were they able
to transform their economies so fundamentally?

Others argue that the fact that Vietnam's capitalism has
unusual features should not be surprising. Rather, the assumption of a single reform path is flawed. The "capitalism-by-de-
sign" model of reform had assumed that old institutions could
be destroyed and completely new kinds of institutions imported
from other contexts to provide the incentives for capitalistic
behavior and integration into the global economy (Sachs 1996).
But countries with such different histories and pre-reform conditions could not be expected to develop the same institutions. In
contrast, the path-dependent transformation model emphasized

that transition institutions are built with the vestiges of previous institutions (Stark 1996). The idea of varieties of capitalisms took hold—market capitalism can incorporate varying levels and types of business-government-labor relations, and supporting institutions can be organized differently in particular societies (Hall and Soskice 2001). The problem with path dependence is that it might suggest that a nation is trapped by its history and that major economic change is not possible except through evolutionary processes so gradual that particular administrations or generations make little impact (Diamond 1999; Pomeranz 2001; Fritsch 2004). But of course that is not true; we have seen cases of major economic reorganization that produced rapid economic growth (Rodrik et al. 2004).

What is well documented but ironically has made little impact on the popularity of free market ideology is that many countries in Asia have seen some of the most remarkably rapid economic development *because* the state played a directive role in the economy. Scholars have suggested that this denial may be in part because revisionist studies try to fit the East Asian miracle economies of an earlier generation into category A when they really belong in category C (Perkins et al. 1995). While the case for the developmental state has been made for the first generation of Asian miracle economies of Japan, South Korea, Taiwan, and Singapore (Evans et al 1985; Amsden 1989), it still needs to be remade for the Asian transition countries because the myth persists that capitalist economies emerge naturally once the state's grabbing hands are tied. For example, while most research cannot help but acknowledge the strong presence of the state in the Chinese economy, it is still primarily viewed as a major structural flaw that will eventually undermine China once the double-digit growth slows down (Lo and Tian 2002; Pei 2006).

While allowing the state back into the market is important in understanding transition, it is only a partial answer. For example, there have been authoritarian states with an export-oriented development agenda whose economies have not grown significantly, and there are also nonauthoritarian, democratic regimes that have grown remarkably (Rodrik and Wacziarg 2005). Moreover, although Vietnam and China have strong states that clearly did not undermine their economic growth, area specialists indicate that while these governments can suppress political opposition and monitor the population, even with all their controlling powers they have had limited ability to actually promote development and transform the economy. Rather, area specialists allude to a widespread social phenomenon behind the rapid economic growth (Fforde and de Vylder 1996; Gainsborough 2003; Ho 2005). The puzzle is this: whether through clever policies or direct state intervention, how does significant change in economic behavior and relations in society happen? Figure 1.1 suggests that there is something missing in our understanding of how major economic system changes occur. If Vietnam did not follow the recommended reforms and the state did not force it, how did the country develop a capitalist economy so quickly?

Beyond New Institutionalism: New Social Cognition Theory

The intellectual stakes involved in solving this puzzle are high. Those debating why some countries transitioned to capitalism more quickly than others often view the world in completely different ways. They also often come from opposite ends of the political spectrum in regard to capitalism. On one side are those who see the world from the point of the individual (agent), viewing economic outcomes as the summation of the choices agents make to serve their best interest. In international development, the agent-based view is often invoked by those who regard the emergence of a capitalist economy as a favorable development because it seems more natural to humans and can produce more wealth. Political stances have become more complex, however, as neoliberal reforms have been embraced by some local intellectuals in transition countries as a strategy to

counter oppressive regimes. In any case, on the other side of
the philosophical spectrum are those whose understanding of
the economy is generated not by individuals but by the larger
social and political forces (structure) that are not the agglom-
erations of individual preferences but have a dynamic of their
own and largely shape the actions of individuals. This position
is often associated with neo-Marxist theories of capitalism that
view structures as created to serve the interests of elites. But it
can also support a leftist position that sees the possibility for
a more positive role for the state in correcting the vagaries of
the market and safeguarding the public's interest, which may be
different from the interests of individuals.

As I conducted this study I was willing to entertain any theory that helps account for the emergence of the new Vietnamese
entrepreneurs and the particular new economic actions they
were making. As I was in the field, I continually tried to test
how much of Vietnam's transition could be explained in terms
of individual agency and how much by structural forces. At the
time, I found that the most helpful theories were in the new
institutionalist literatures in economics, sociology, and political
science, which were working to reconcile the long-standing tension between structure and agency in order to explain changes
in and variations between economies.

New institutional economics seemed to be a particularly promising development because it was having an impact on international development policy discourse. Since institutions, defined as
"humanly devised constraints that structure political, economic,
and social interaction" by North (1991), vary between countries,
they might account for why markets emerge more quickly in some
places than in others. While this might seem obviously sensible,
it was an important step in development thinking because some
contemporary Adam Smiths still espouse the naturalness of capitalism based on the human desire to profit (Pipes 1996). Instead,
institutionalists argued that agents only make choices that have
been made feasible or reasonable by social institutions. In other
words, capitalists need the help of an array of institutions to facilitate their activities. The real-world costs of finding one another,

obtaining information, conducting negotiations, and calculating transaction risks could be inhibiting economic transactions (Williamson 1996). Perhaps the key for developing and transitioning economies was to build institutions, including government institutions, that support entrepreneurial activity (Coase 1992). This concept was accepted by the mainstream development organizations and their projects were increasingly directed toward "capacity building" and "institutional development." However, institutions were usually conceived of narrowly as establishing the rule of law, especially private property rights legislation, strengthening courts for contract enforcement, and reforming bank financing, all of which were integral to the original liberalization reforms that we observed had limited impact. But there is another question.

Can one really build an institution by announcing it and funding it? Economists have well-developed analytic methods to measure the impact of preexisting institutions on economic transactions. But ideas about institutional change have been underdeveloped. It has primarily been conceived as occurring in response to changes in the costs and benefits of the economic environment (Demsetz 1967). Society, acting as a single actor made up of individual optimizing agents, chooses the most efficient institutional design.[2]

Many sociologists and political scientists have severely criticized economics' conception of institutions and human behavior. They have argued that people's economic actions are not motivated solely by their narrow economic self-interest but are heavily influenced by what other people do and by the desire to be social, as well as to exert power over others. In other words, institutions that allow capitalist economies to function are the result of a social process rather than an agglomeration of individual choices. Sociological studies of firms and entrepreneurs have shown that group power interests, identity, social norms, social networks, and culture are important factors in explaining economic outcomes that cannot be explained with truncated behavioral assumptions (DiMaggio and Powell 1983; Saxenian 1996; Granovetter 2005).

Furthermore, sociologists do not think of institutions as just exogenous forces but rather as embedded in the agents, who help to reproduce them. This implies that one society's institutions would have a different social meaning in another society and thus cannot simply be exported, which might help to explain the ineffectiveness of some reform efforts. Thick structuralists go as far to say that agents are not always fully conscious of how they have been conditioned by society to play certain roles. A person's freedom to choose actions in her interest is compromised by structures that have been formed to support a social system. For example, Bourdieu has documented the difficult and major cognitive shift Algerians undertook to adapt to colonial France's market mentality. He showed how the structural forces took away their freedom to make choices in their best interest because even their aspirations had been colonized, which reified their lower social position through their dispositions and actions (Bourdieu 1997).

But, while power and politics shape economic institutions, these factors are not enough to account for the outcomes of transition economies. Thick structuralists and neo-Marxists would have predicted that the former political elites would transform their political capital into the new economic capital. In Central Europe, however, the old Communist Party members have tended to not benefit economically. Rather it was the young and better educated, as well as those who were able to form alliances with the new politocracy and opinion-making intellectual elites, who tended to become wealthier (Svejnar 1996). It appears that in Central Europe's new capitalism, cultural capital produced the greatest financial returns. Describing Central Europe as "capitalism without capitalists," Eyal, Szelenyi, and Townsley (1998) argue that these countries developed market institutions without a propertied bourgeoisie.[3] Nee (1989) also found that at the beginning of transition in China, cadre members who acted entrepreneurially might initially enjoy market power but the financial returns declined as the market expanded. In contrast to the Eyal, Szelenyi, and Townsley study, Nee found that formal education was not a significant form of the new cultural capital that produced economic benefits (Nee 1996). In any case, because of these outcomes, some argue that we need to move beyond the Marxist model of capitalism that supposed economies transitioned to capitalism in order to support the material interests of elites (Nee and Swedberg 2007).

To be able to account for diversity in economic outcomes such as this, other sociologists, such as Granovetter, advocate for a social theory that retains some agency, as opposed to the views of "over-socialized sociologists" who suggest that people are slavishly programmed to follow roles. While broad historical and macro-structural circumstances do shape agents, people are still capable of purposeful actions (Granovetter 1985). This does not imply that one must espouse the rational agent model; rather, agents form relationships and social networks that mediate an agent's action to act purely in her self-interest. Through these actions and interactions, social norms and structures are constructed and reconstructed. Meanwhile, structuralists criticize "interactionists" such as Granovetter, arguing that they do not distinguish between agents within a system who operate within different sets of networks or exhibit different economic aspirations as a result of larger structural forces (Burawoy 2001; Collet 2003; Bourdieu 2005). The core disagreement has been about whether issues of power and inequality are adequately addressed in a perspective that is more concerned with the mechanics of how social factors influence economic actions.

Despite these differences, the general trend toward focusing on institutions in a variety of disciplines at the end of the twentieth century was exciting and promising for several reasons. Leading scholars in different disciplines all acknowledged that institutions such as laws, though seemingly set in stone, are actually socially constructed. The socially constructed nature of institutions should help to explain the observed variation in capitalisms and economic outcomes. Furthermore, it implies that they can be reconstructed and therefore that change is possible. But the disparate new institutionalist literatures in economics, sociology, and political science have had problems communicating with one another. One obstacle is that they have fundamentally different human behavioral models with respect to what motivates actions: innate self-interest or socially shaped interests. At the millennium, scholars from several disciplines recognized the need for the social sciences' equivalent of a unifying theory outlining the relationship between institutions and individuals. Granovetter (2002) summed it up well when he proposed that this theory needs to integrate how social norms, instrumental self-interest, trust, and power jointly motivate and shape economic action. Furthermore, this theory needs to be dynamic enough to explain institutional change.

The new institutionalist literature has been weak in explaining how economies have changed, especially with respect to the more recent phenomenon of transition economies. Given the overwhelming number of ineffective economic reform policies and programs, a central question for international development concerns how significant economic change happens. Toward this end, this study asks, How is it that some transition economies were able to develop active, capitalistic economies so quickly? What enabled the fundamental, society-wide change from a centrally planned economy to the fastest growing markets in the world? Understanding institutional change requires us to reconsider what motivates a change in behavior by moving beyond ideas of narrow self-interest and submission to domination.

Exciting points of convergence are now emerging across the disciplines that can lead us out of the disparate new institutionalisms and better illuminate the process of institutional change. The most recent research acknowledges the critical role cognition plays in explaining changes in behavior and recognizes that changes in cognition are socially constructed. This new social cognition perspective helps account for the diversity of outcomes between the transition economies.

Social Cognition and Institutional Change

Studying the role of cognition in institutional change is a major development for the social sciences and an important step forward out of the structure-versus-agency dilemma. If we acknowledge that cognition needs to be studied, the implication is that we must no longer assume a universal behavioral model. This challenges the sufficiency of both the free market and developmental state models of economic development. Ironically, in both models, people and society are rather passive objects that can be acted upon. In the free market paradigm, society resembles a hospital patient who is prescribed a set of policies with cleverly designed incentives to harness the innate human desire for self-benefit—a type of social engineering. Policymakers check the vital signs before and after a policy intervention with outcome indicators such as GDP growth rates, but do not look at the internal functions. Meanwhile, political economy accounts focus on the state and political elites, who desire to gain and maintain dominance and who rather easily manipulate or goad the rest of society into new economic relations. In either case, people's underlying motivations are simple and homogeneous. While either theory can provide powerful insights into a subset of cases, they both lack explanatory power to describe the range of outcomes observed in developing and transition economies.

Now, institutionalists are no longer assuming universal and unchanging conceptions of human interest. The way to account for the diversity observed within and between economies is to recognize that the motivations behind economic actions are multifaceted and malleable. The objective, then, is to understand how they are formed and how they change in order to lead to new behaviors such as entrepreneurialism.

The latest literature reveals a renewed appreciation that our interests are socially constructed and that they can be reconstructed. There is also a growing recognition that this construction project happens in the cognitive realm. Returning to social construction processes as the source of institutional variation and the cognitive realm as the connection between social structure and human agency provides the more general framework necessary to explain the diversity of observed outcomes. The turn toward the social construction of cognition, or social cognition, engages fields of research that are new to international development discourse, such as developmental psychology and the newly forming cognitive institutional economics and cognitive sociology.

The idea of social cognition in the social sciences is not new, however. Berger and Luckman's classic *The Social Construction of Reality* (1967) proposed that institutions were actually first created in our minds. Agents interacting together in a social system form a new mental paradigm of their and others' roles and expected behaviors. As these reciprocal roles become embedded with meaning in the social fabric, this knowledge is made into material facts through action. In other words, the difference between real institutional change and ineffectual and irrelevant reforms depends on whether new ideas have entered people's consciousness and been absorbed into social relations so that they become expected and normal and people behave accordingly. The key to understanding meaningful institutional change is to examine the cognitive paradigm shifts taking place in society.

Sociologists have long been concerned with how social structures interact with human cognition. What is surprising is that some economists are now seriously entertaining cognitive issues.[4] Greif is an important scholar in this regard, introducing new directions in institutional economics while also collaborating with sociologists (Greif 2005). International development policy usually assumes respect for new laws and policies. Greif astutely posits that when economists point to rules and laws as institutions because they affect agent behavior through enforcement, they only push the real question back to what is motivating the behavior of the enforcer. There is a larger dynamic making both agent and enforcer interact by the rules. He names norms, beliefs, and culture as the microfoundation institutions that shape agent motivations for following rule-based institutions; that is the reason enforcers enforce the rules. He also acknowledges that institutions can change endogenously.

Douglass North, the father of new institutional economics, has also advocated the cognitive turn. He confines the rational choice paradigm to a certain subset of inquiry (competitive market situations). But in times of major institutional change involving novel situations, multiple agents, collective action, and high uncertainty, even the most rational of agents can no longer follow his or her usual decision-making processes. Agents have to learn new paradigms (Denzau and North 1994). North makes the case that economists need to further develop a model of "cognitive institutionalism" in order to understand the process of economic system change (Mantzavinos, North, and Shariq 2004; North 2005).

These economists, however, have been limited to adopting a particular branch of cognitive science literature. Although North does not acknowledge Piaget explicitly, he essentially employs the dominant theory in developmental psychology, the Piagetian principles of equilibration: cognitive change happens because human beings are adaptive organisms who try to reconcile observations of our environment that clash with our current cognitive paradigms. Piaget significantly advanced behavioral psychology, which previously did not examine internal mental states because they were not "real," or at least not susceptible to analysis. Piagetian theorists view humans as organisms that by definition constantly change, including their cognitive frameworks which shift to construct new meaning and knowledge as a way to order changes in their environment (Goldhaber 2000). But Piaget's framework is still a single agent model perspective: an individual actor is trying to reconcile new observations of external stimuli.

This is precisely one of the reasons sociologists have historically had an aversion to psychological research. Some sociologists resist considering cognition as a construct because they assume its framework requires an independent agent and is limited to experimental positivism. But the emerging school of cognitive sociology recognizes that psychology has moved away from the behaviorism of the 1950s. In fact, cross-cultural empirical research in the contextual branch of the cognitive development literature has provided evidence that there are very few universal psychological processes, in part because human development is so intimately tied to how societies make meaning of their world in a particular historical place and time. About a hundred years ago, Vygotzky posited that society teaches agents not only what to think but *how* to think (1978).

For example, an interesting recent study combined anthropological fieldwork with behavioral experiments. A team of researchers set out across the world to ask members of different societies to play the classic prisoner's dilemma economics game. Their findings show societies play the game of self-interest differently and that the same game plays mean something different in various societies because of the ways in which they relate to their everyday economic practices (Henrich, Boyd et al. 2004). Bandura (1986), who first coined the term social cognition, presented compelling evidence that changes in human behavior are not decided by an individualistic agent whose actions are primarily governed by biological or other natural impulses. Recent advances in cognitive research can be used to confirm and further detail the mechanisms of the social construction process (DiMaggio 1997; Zerubavel 1997).

Power and Social Cognition

While the cognitive development literature provides important insights into the processes of changing social cognition, it has not adequately addressed issues of power or social conflict, even though these are key to institutional change. That is, institutions and economic outcomes also vary because they require the involvement of a variety of members within a society, and this interplay, which can unfold in a number of ways, requires investigation. Structuralists have derided past sociological attempts to conceptualize the mental realm by reducing culture to shared values, norms, and attitudes rather than viewing culture as a resource that is put to strategic use by elites (DiMaggio 1997). However, the *new* social cognition theory distinguishes itself from psychology's original social cognition theory in its explicit analysis of how power dynamics in society reshape cognition.

The incorporation of power into social cognition theory is helped by the increasingly diminishing divide between thick structuralists and interactionists. Granovetter's more recent publications have incorporated power and alliances into his social network analysis. Using the history of electricity pricing in the United States, Granovetter and colleagues demonstrate how powerful figures in the industry used their influence to shape the formation of pricing regimes toward their interests in ways that efficiency and short-term profit incentives alone would not have predicted (Granovetter, Yakubovich, and McGuire 2005). Meanwhile, Bourdieu, in a posthumously published work, examines institutional change rather than uncovering the forces behind institutional stasis (2005). While not deviating from his emphasis on the importance of power and social positions, he identifies individuals and the relationships they form in order to explain why the French housing market structure privileges a particular housing type—single family houses. Both accounts appeal to processes of social reconstruction.

More recent treatments of power appreciate that the most powerful individuals and groups in society have a limit on how much they can coerce society into normalizing change. At some point, those the powerful are trying to influence also contribute to the process of institutional adoption. As the transition cases have shown, sometimes the powerful were not able to retain their power and did not benefit economically in transition. Current frameworks examine not only power but the resistance to power as part of an ongoing social reconstruction process. And part of this negotiation of power happens in the cognitive realm, as the less powerful contribute to the stream of sociocultural knowledge that provides critiques on the limitations and legitimacy of power and can fuel acts of resistance and ultimately institutional change (Silbey and Ewick 2003). Thus the new social construction approach dwells on power's limits.

Yet the empirical studies of power in transition economies have tended to focus on the most powerful, almost completely ignoring others. Scholars such as Burawoy have criticized "trendy sociologists" who privilege entrepreneurs and elites by making them the object of study when the old Marxist criticisms of bureaucracy domination and the marginalized underclass are still relevant (Burawoy 2001). I not only agree that class issues still matter in understanding transition, but I also see it as unavoidable in light of the spreading and sometimes violent struggles over land control by farmers and the displaced who are moved by the state to make room for the new urban developments of entrepreneurs in the Asian transition countries. We should expand our examination to include the less powerful agents involved in the social construction project. In the study of transition to market capitalisms, one has to analyze not only firms and entrepreneurs, the state and bureaucracy, but also their interactions with consumers and those who are being displaced.

The direction toward new social cognition theory offers a more comprehensive framework to the disjointed combination of new institutionalist theories that became popular during the 1980s and 90s. It suggests that the chasm in the structure-versus-agency dilemma can be bridged by focusing on how society shapes agent cognition and how agents resist and negotiate power in society. This integrative direction has gained the attention of the present scholarship on the institutional foundations of capitalism (Greif 2006; Nee and Swedberg 2007; North 2005). *Learning to Be Capitalists* further elaborates this theoretical direction by examining the details of how Vietnam's first generation of entrepreneurs emerged, despite conventional wisdom. It examines the cognitive shifts that took place in them and in society and the power struggles that took place to negotiate the new cognitive paradigms and the ultimate shape of Vietnam's capitalist institutions. The concepts of social cognition provide missing pieces to the transition puzzle.

The Research

Vietnam is a particularly important case for explaining the puzzle of variation among the transition economies. While China has garnered much more ink and scrutiny, Vietnam's transition is more surprising in many ways. It is a relatively small country that could not command the level of interest from foreign direct investment that China could (Hsing 1998); it started off poorer and less resourced, and yet by some measures it has transitioned more quickly.

Even while Vietnam has grown rapidly, policy circles have consistently viewed it as backward in terms of an institutional framework necessary to support a market economy (IMF 2000; Heritage Foundation 2004). In particular, although it has an authoritarian state it does not resemble the kind of developmental state that characterized the Asian miracle economies of an earlier generation (Japan, South Korea, and Singapore). Instead, its central government has allowed local governments to exercise considerable discretion in implementing economic policies.

The Asian transition cases are also important because of their different institutional paths. Although Greif (2006) explicitly points to the existence of multiple equilibria, also known as varieties of capitalism, his substantive findings attribute the West's rise in economic power to a particular set of micro-foundations: individualism, self-governance with weak states during feudalism, and non-kinship organizations such as the church. He argues that this institutional inheritance contributed to the emergence of the modern corporation. The danger is that his findings can be misinterpreted to imply that particular cultural histories and traits are needed to promote capitalism. Unlike western Europe, the Asian transition countries generally do not have individualistic cultures and do have histories of kinship organizations before Communism, as well as strong central governments. The Asian economies' rapid rise is in obvious contradiction to the exigency of Western institutions.

In order to unravel the puzzle of Vietnam's transition, this book starts with what is new: the emergence of new economic actors and their actions. In particular, I focus in on the newly emerged private housing market in HCMC and the entrepreneurs who direct the new private land development firms. Since none of this existed ten years before my study began, I focused on finding how these particular entrepreneurs emerged.

The new land developers and housing market in HCMC make an ideal case for study because the situation lends itself to comparative analysis, through which we can further test the applicability of the social cognition model. For example, private land development firms did not emerge in Hanoi. While both markets are within the same country and share many constants, such as the formal political and legal institutions and the basic high housing demand, will we find social cognition as a plausible explanation for this disparity? This book also makes some comparative observations with private land developers in Warsaw, Poland. One might want to attribute the emergence of indigenous real estate firms to the conventional transition policies Poland pursued. But if we directly consult Warsaw's entrepreneurs and real estate industry analysts, will we find that these reforms were really the causal factors behind a private housing market? Is there any similarity between what happened in Warsaw's transition and what happened in HCMC? Thirdly, while much has been written about China's urban transition, will we find similar social, cognitive forces at play in both of these maverick transition cases?

One might ask if the real estate industry is a suitable sector for comparing the transitions to capitalism. For one thing, it is not an export industry. But this does not mean that it is immune to the pressures of global capital investment. In fact, not only was land the physical platform for new enterprises at the beginning of transition, but land, because it is fixed and tangible, was the initial investment of choice in an unstable economic environment in many transition economies. Investment analysts in Vietnam refer to real estate as one of the key sectors in Vietnam's recent economic expansion that contributed to domestic demand and money supply (Mekong Capital 2007). It is a core industry in developed market economies as well, where real estate represents 45–70 percent of a nation's assets (Ibbotson, Siegel, and Love 1985). In addition to being an investment vehicle, land development is foundational to the building of capitalism. Surveys of Vietnamese businesses indicate that finding land for their productive activities is one of the most challenging parts of setting up operations and also one of the major constraints on their future growth.[5] Property markets are also a relevant sector in which to discuss larger aspects of the transition to capitalism since the advice given to the real estate industries of transition economies mirrors the conventional free-market advice given to these countries more generally. Specifically, policy reformers focus on strengthening and enforcing legal property rights, deregulation, selling state assets, and developing housing finance institutions. Accordingly, in addition to the low rankings of their other economic institutions (IMF 2000; Heritage Foundation 2004), Vietnam has continually been ranked as having the worst institutional framework for private real estate investment among 56 countries (Jones Lang LaSalle 2006). Therefore, among Vietnam's various economic sectors, the land development industry is one that is core to its transition mystery.

Methods

The study of capitalism (and Communism) is an ideological minefield filled with caricatures. Although it is impossible to be perfectly objective, the intent of this study was to be empirical, documenting and analyzing the phenomenon almost anthropologically. My entrée was the new entrepreneurs. Entrepreneurs fascinate development institutions, but few really take the time to meet them and learn what they do.

When I first arrived in HCMC and began meeting developers, I tried to sit them down to test my pilot survey instrument, peppering them with questions about project dates, number of housing units, costs, and so forth. It quickly became apparent that this type of formal inquiry did not work with the way the entrepreneurs operate, nor with the context. For one thing, it was difficult to collect data for a survey as developers were busy fielding calls on their cell phones. On the other hand I would have missed the great deal of consequential time they spent leisurely socializing and visiting people. But there was also a more serious problem: I was restricting my analysis too

narrowly. By limiting my observation to questions about existing concepts of institutions such as transaction costs, networks,
norms, and rules, I could not address the larger question of how
all of these factors were embodied in the developers and were
motivating a change in behavior and roles. In other words, my
research question, asking how these entrepreneurs emerged and
developed projects, involves basic research: reconceptualizing
models and entertaining new variables. Since neither *homo eco-
nomicus*, developmental state, power conversion, nor evolutionary models satisfactorily account for the variety we have seen in
transition economies and in particular the kind of structured,
decentralized, and abrupt entrepreneurialism present in HCMC,
I was searching for a new framework.

Some have advocated the use of game theory analytics to
study the role of cognition in institutional change (Greif 2006). It
can be helpful in providing a systematic way to compare strategies and outcomes. One problem with using game theory in
cross-cultural settings, however, is that because its framework
attributes motivations theorized a priori to observed behavior,
one could miss the socialized meaning of the action (Loewenstein
1999; Henrich, Boyd et al. 2004). In some contexts, splitting
resources in half is not fair but generous or stingy. In addition,
the researcher may be affecting experiment outcomes by the way
they frame questions and the options they give the subject—that
is, we cannot be sure how the subject is interpreting the rules of
the game. Others argue that the way people play games may not
reflect how they live everyday life (Garfinkel 1967).

An alternative to experiments, games, and surveys is fieldwork. In particular, the extended case study method can be used
to rebuild our understanding when we examine an anomaly that
challenges previous theories (Burawoy 1998). Through multiple,
open-ended interviews and through participant observation, the
researcher can move through space and time with the subject
to gain insight to meaning and processes.[6] Intellectual avenues
opened once I spent less time asking questions and more time
listening to the developers tell me what they thought they were
doing. Equally important were watching how they interacted

with others and living in HCMC to observe them in the larger context of their society. I kept trying to put my finger on the rich phenomenon I was observing that was not addressed by the new institutionalist literature I had read before coming to Vietnam. Ultimately, the study led me to this book's thesis on the role of cognition and power in the social reconstruction of the economy.

Studying something as ephemeral as changing social cognition requires a careful consideration of methods. Narrative analysis is a useful way to understand how individuals understand and relate to social structures. The stories people tell indicate a society's shared schema, rather than a personal one, because otherwise they would be unintelligible to their listener (Silbey and Ewick 2003). Garfinkel (1967) champions "lay sociologists," such as my developers, who can locate for us their practical theories about why people in their world behave as they do.

Of course, the ethnographer still views the situation through her own mental structures, cultural biases, and foci of attention. And the subject's accounts may have been altered by interacting with me, a foreign woman. My respondents seemed to tell their stories partly out of amusement that I should be interested, as well as from a sense of recording history, esteeming scholarship. They explained how they thought things worked in their changing society, allowing me to locate shared explanations, sentiments, and themes. I did very little talking except to clarify and test my comprehension of what they were telling me through counterfactual scenarios and triangulation of respondents. Some consider ethnographic data to be too "soft" compared to numbers that can be coded into a computer. But the advantage of using contemporary fieldwork is that the researcher can engage in dialogue with the phenomenon of study—we can ask the entrepreneurs questions about their motivations and spend time with them in their institutional environment to get a first-hand sense of what their acts signify, as well as more readily allowing them to contradict our understanding.

When I began to seek out some entrepreneurs and find out what they were doing, I needed to first invest considerable time in HCMC and Vietnam to familiarize myself with this atypical market and formulate definitions for even such basic concepts as "private firm" when the state owns all land, requires detailed monitoring of its activities, and often has government employees as investors in its private projects. After initial fieldwork, I found that there were four different types of private land development firms operating in HCMC, including the loose, "investor group" type, which are unregistered with the government and which I would not have known to survey before the fieldwork.

The approach I took was to narrow down, extremely, the unit of analysis and to open as wide as possible the detection of explanatory factors. I selected 14 case firms that were working in the urban periphery of one city in one transition country. These cases included the four firm types and varied in size and productivity. I studied them because they were willing to be studied—I was able to get unusual access to and candid interviews with the entrepreneurs in these firms. The units of analysis for the study were the new economic actions of these entrepreneurs. Observed changes in actions are important; while changes may happen officially on one level and resources may be poured into "institutional capacity building" projects, these policies and projects may have little impact in wider society. Rather than the usual route of assuming policies were important per se and trying to detect any outcomes from policies, I reversed the order and identified significant new economic acts and then found the factors and processes that were important in their emergence. After investment in the field, I identified four key economic actions made by the developers—steps that were crucial to their ability to convert agricultural land into residential land for sale in HCMC's new housing market: 1) finding developable land, 2) negotiating land compensation with current occupants, 3) obtaining permits and approvals from the various bureaucracies to develop a specific land parcel, and 4) finding development financing.

While I have just discussed the necessity of qualitative methods for this study, I am actually ecumenical about research methods. For example, in chapter 6 I employ standard hedonic price models with thousands of observations to show how norms were operationalized into market prices. But the heart of this book is the fourteen months of ethnographic research I conducted, which were spread over six years, the majority occurring during 2000 and 2001. The hours I spent interviewing the developers, visiting their project sites, meeting their associates in the private sector and in government, socializing with their friends, and observing how they interacted with others provided rich data that could not be confined in a survey or experiments.

The material in the book is organized in two sections. I start with the entrepreneurs and their new behaviors. In the next chapter, we will see that these entrepreneurs required many networks and relationships in order to navigate their highly structured economic environment. In chapter 3, I compare those entrepreneurs who were highly successful and productive with those who were not, and find that the differences between them include the agency they displayed in learning to develop projects and the institutions they created. These two chapters suggest that concepts of both agency and structure need to be better integrated in order to understand the emergence and particular activities of these entrepreneurs. The second section of the book focuses on the processes of institutional change. We see in chapter 4 that the developers' new ideas about their economic roles and acceptable actions changed in conjunction with a larger social power struggle that included those with varying levels and sources of power: local state actors, new housing consumers, and displaced farmers. The fifth chapter presents how social cognition theory better explains this study's empirical findings about the emergence and activities of HCMC's entrepreneurs than conventional development theories. In chapter 6, I further build the case for social cognition theory by showing how it helps us unravel mysteries of transition such as the lack of entrepreneurs in Hanoi and the emergence of private land developers in places as different as Poland and China. We find that a widespread reconstruction of social cognition is necessary in order to enable the very material transfers of property ownership in society that under-gird the new capitalism. There is no teacher. Society learns to be capitalist on its own terms.

Notes

1. Although I first call the city Saigon as a way to convey familiarity and because it is what locals often still call the city, for the rest of the book I will usually refer to it as Ho Chi Minh City, abbreviated HCMC.

2. Richard Nelson (2002) has also proposed joining institutional eco-nomics with evolutionary economics to explain how institutions change by using Darwinian concepts of the variation, replication, and selection of "social technologies" through processes of individual and collective learn-ing. Some of these processes share some affinities with what is presented in this book, but Nelson's approach is still fundamentally different in its agen-tic perspective that does not articulate the social and political processes.

3. Meanwhile, they summarize Russia as a case of capitalists without capi-talism, where an oligarchy enriched themselves by easily grabbing property and stripping state assets in an economic environment without competitive market institutions (Eyal, Szelenyi, and Townsley 1998).

4. Behavioral economics has also gained significant interest in the eco-nomics literature, but its research has primarily been applied to finance. Mullainathan has recently explored possible connections to international development and policymaking (2007), although he stays within the agentic perspective.

5. The findings of two recent business surveys are cited in a special issue of a bulletin issued by the Vietnam Chamber of Commerce and Industry (2007). One was jointly conducted by the Mekong Private Sector Development Facility and the Foreign Investment Advisory Service of the International Finance Corporation, and the second was commissioned by German Technical Cooperation (GTZ) and Vietnam's Central Institute of Economic Management.

6. It so happens that ethnographic research is the chief method contex-tualist schools of cognitive psychology employ in cross-cultural research (Rogoff 1990). Observing agents in situ is a more appropriate way to exam-ine how larger social structures shape cognitive processes. Because the same actions can mean something different in different contexts, research-ers need to immerse themselves in the local context to ascertain a sense of the meaning.

Part I

The New Entrepreneurs

2

To Become an Entrepreneur in Ho Chi Minh City

Sociability, Networks, and Political Connections

"I know where you were this morning," the leader of one of the largest land development companies in HCMC told me. I was startled by this revelation, since I had not told him I had been interviewing another company that morning. I was not aware of any connection between the two companies because I had been introduced to them through different people. It was easy for foreign researchers to succumb to paranoia in Vietnam's restrictive research environment, but my informant relieved me of that concern with his cavalier forthrightness. Even though we had just met, he told me that he was an unofficial vice-director of the smaller company. He also explained the links of ownership between this large firm and several other companies, the percentage of government ownership in their company, how the industry was organized, and the political interests behind the networks.

Later that year, I arranged a meeting between one of my case firms and a group from the World Bank on a reconnaissance mission to recommend housing finance development projects to Vietnam. They were impressed by the professionalism and efficiency of the firm's staff. These Vietnamese seemed like the quintessential new capitalists. One of the older consultants commented to me, with gleaming eyes, "This is the future..." Meanwhile, I was struck again by the people who had shown up for our meeting. What he did not realize were all of the actors behind this meeting we had just had: the array of people who knew about it before it happened, the loose confederation of people who had come together to make the presentations, and the intricate web of people who keep projects in the company's pipeline.

Experiences like this throughout my time in HCMC made it obvious that in this market, the land developers are extensively networked and the state is intimately involved, especially with the largest companies. These accounts contradict the myth of the rugged, lone entrepreneur whose own personality traits and taste for risk have led to his new activities. In Vietnam, at least, investigating how the entrepreneurs could conduct business led to studying the other people with whom they worked.

Traditionally, one would think of such close relationships between firms, and between firms and government, as collusive and undesirable for a number of reasons. The lack of competition could lead to a wasteful use of resources and higher market prices, rendering housing out of reach for more people. It could also increase wealth inequality and inefficiency by giving special investment opportunities to those with political connections. Other literature, however, has emphasized the crucial role the state has always played in the formation of market economies by supporting specific firms (Amsden 1989; Evans 1995). Rather than thinking of capitalism as a natural outcome of individual interactions, we should recognize that capitalism requires the active participation of the state. Indeed, the lack of effective state engagement might help to explain why so many developing countries have not grown more rapidly. Furthermore, social networks within an industry have been identified as an important determinant of successful economic outcomes in the global economy because they can be important conduits for spreading market information, especially in developing industries (Saxenian 1996). While networks need to be strong enough to engender information sharing, in the more successful markets they also need to be open enough to new members to allow new information to enter and impel corrections and adaptations (Granovetter 1983). Social norms have also been used as a substitute for law in regulating economic transactions and enforcing contracts through peer pressure and reputation incentives (Ellickson 1991). But scholars argue whether such substitutions are sustainable in large, urban communities where social ties are reformed and social sanctions are not binding (Ellickson 1993). Nevertheless, Woodruff and McMillan found that firms in transition countries were able to create new trading partners beyond their original social networks without strong legal institutions, and that in Vietnam informal contracts between firms and their suppliers were prevalent, even though they were not practically enforceable by courts (Woodruff and McMillan 1999, 2002). Thus, there is disagreement in the literature about how to view the necessity and desirability of networks and political connections in market operations.

In the case of HCMC, political connections and social networks permeated all of the activities of the entrepreneurs. This is necessarily so because the state still retains considerable oversight of the economy and controls land use, so much so that most experts have assessed Vietnam as an impossible place to invest. It would be impossible if one were to follow a textbook model of business decision making. In order to appreciate the challenging economic environment in which the entrepreneurs were operating and why social networks and political connections were an important part of their work, this chapter first describes the large role the state has played in structuring the land development industry.

However, while the ability to work with the government was a prerequisite, political connections did not determine who became entrepreneurs. As other studies have found, those with political capital during the era of central planning did not necessarily become the new financial capitalists or fare well economically in transition. To address this issue, the remainder of the chapter makes observations about the social position of the first generation of land developers and where they came from. The next chapter will present a more detailed explanation of how they expanded their networks and found ways to work within the structural constraints and why some became more successful than others.

Constraints in the Economic Environment

"It's all about the land," explained one key informant with steady eyes, early on in my fieldwork. I came to understand that as probably the single truest statement about real estate in Vietnam.

The prices for land started skyrocketing during the 1990–93 period. Firm #8's leader recalls, "Individuals were buying and selling land. In the morning you could make a deposit of 8 oz. of gold per square meter and in the afternoon you could already sell it for 30 oz. A few days later the price could be 200 oz. You could make a big profit in one project; pay 1 oz. of gold and sell at 700 oz." The 1986 *doi moi* reform policies introducing Vietnam's economic sea change had gained unstoppable momentum. Now that people were officially allowed to buy commodities instead of receiving rations, population migration to cities and private trading increased. Although the 1993 Land Law, which first officially allowed the concept of private real property rights into the economy, had not yet been instituted, private land sales were occurring in a frenzy.[1] Thus the law did not unleash the market, but rather signaled that the state would now allow it as it had in other transition cases (Gold and Bonnell 2002).

With the skyrocketing land prices, fortunes could be made, and were being made. The key was to find land that was undervalued because it was still at the beginning of the rapid appreciation curve and cheap enough to buy with one's own pool of financial capital and that of fellow investors. Besides flipping raw land back onto the market, even greater gains could be had by holding onto the land long enough to subdivide it into parcels and develop infrastructure and housing. The high demand for urban land created strong financial incentives for people to invest in land development projects.

But profit also depended on the ability to control the costs of development. The successful, professional firms explained it to me literally as a formula: land purchase costs could range anywhere from 30–50% of the total development cost; around 50–60% of costs were used for construction, primarily infrastructure development, and the remainder was spent on fees such as land taxes. Since construction costs are standard and taxes are fixed, the biggest variable for profit was the cost involved in obtaining land use rights. It was also the most critical, since the site's location provides most of the value to real estate.

The variability in land costs included the financial payment as well as the time it took to negotiate and make the agreement stick. Usually project sites in urban and peri-urban areas involve land that is already occupied by other citizens, so purchasing land rights entails compensating the current occupants to move off the land. In the urban periphery of HCMC during the early years of transition, these were usually farmers, because the land had previously been designated for agricultural use. Not surprisingly, with huge potential gains hinging on this transfer, everyone interviewed concurred that agreeing on land compensation was by far the most difficult step in project development, which is why it was "all about the land."

This struggle for land control was not a private matter. The state shaped the context in which this land transfer was taking place, in both direct and indirect ways. Through state ownership, annexation, master planning, and the distribution of land use rights, the state determined where land conversion for private development could happen and the terms of transfer.

State Ownership of Land and the Stability
of Property Rights

In Vietnam, one of the major pillars of the Communist revolution is that the state owns all land. However, during the economic transition toward a market economy, the state introduced
private land use rights for a specific period of time, similar to
China. For noncommercial holders of residential property, the
right extends in perpetuity. For commercial entities, land use
rights usually last for 25 years.[2]

To those accustomed to freehold land tenure systems, use
rights might seem too weak a private property right to under-
pin commercial investment in real estate. Other mature market
economies, such as Hong Kong and the United Kingdom, however, show that it is possible for leasehold land tenure systems
to essentially function as private property rights for commercial investment (Bourassa and Hong 2003). But in Vietnam, the
government not only owns all land in name but also directly
controls much of the supply of developable land. As some of
my case firms and key informants describe the situation, the
private firms are allowed to get the leftover parcels of land that
are not already being developed by the state.

Although it was not possible to obtain exact figures on all
public landholdings in the urban periphery of HCMC, several
key informants estimated that the state and state-owned enterprises control about 50% of the land in the periphery designated
for residential development in the city's master plan. One of the
largest of these is RESCO, a city-owned group that in 2001 consisted of 17 real estate companies and related services companies. In the beginning of transition, all private investors had to
purchase land directly from RESCO. Of the roughly 44,000 hectares of land in the urban periphery I studied, between 1994 and
2000 RESCO developed 237 residential projects on 4,382 hectares
of land, producing 135,216 units. RESCO had development control rights for 5000 more hectares, but only 1,664 hectares had
even vaguely described projects planned for them. Of the 115
residential projects proposed, 88 had cost estimates that would

require 3.45 trillion VND (roughly $238 million USD) in capital to develop them. With a net profit of 61 billion VND in 2000, RESCO clearly does not have the capital to fund these projects. In press interviews, RESCO representatives said that "the rest is to be mobilized from the community and various economic sectors" (Hong 2000). So while the state has a monopoly on land supply in HCMC, it needs the financial participation of the private sector.

But private participation was not forthcoming in the beginning of the transition period. Firm #1 reported that it was still risky to buy land for fear of state expropriation without fair compensation. Economic theory would suggest that because property rights were not very well articulated in the law or enforced by the court system that was still undeveloped and backlogged with cases, private land development organizations were inhibited from investing in land. Most of the firms I studied, however, had actively begun developing projects by 1998 and 1999, before further developments in the Land Law were released in 2003. And the majority of annual new housing was privately supplied by at least 1994 (HCMC Statistical Yearbook 1997).

While expropriation was still possible, it no longer had the same chilling effect on investment by the late 1990s. For one thing, firms observed the state's greater effort to limit arbitrary expropriation with the public display of master plans and more compensation for expropriation of urban land. For example, the state expropriated about one-half of Firm #2's project site in the Phuoc Long B ward of District 9 to build a road. The firm had originally bought this farmland in 1996 for 90,000 VND/sqm, and the state compensated them 60,000 VND/sqm. Firm #2's leader stated: "Before, the compensation rate was much lower. Compensation is always lower than the market price, but the price we received is acceptable because no infrastructure has been developed yet." He did not complain of lost opportunity costs. Rather, he considered the lower compensation rate reasonable, and the company was able to recoup its losses by the rapid increase in value of the remaining area of land it still owned, which now had better transportation access. Expropriation also became less of a risk when firms found ways to avoid the situation and locate sites with low likelihood of expropriation through better information about public investment plans.

In addition to limiting state expropriation, well enforced and documented private property rights are supposed to support investment by reducing risks coming from other private citizens through multiple ownership claims and boundary disputes. While these do occur in Vietnam, they are not at a level that inhibited the formation of a market. Ironically, a large part of the stability of Vietnam's property rights situation comes from state ownership of land. The government exerts an overarching authority over all land use conversions, as official private land transactions involve an intervening step of returning the land use right back to the state. Furthermore, during the era of central planning, households were registered and not allowed much mobility, a situation that ended up providing an alternate means of documented tenancy at the beginning of transition. With such information, the extensive Communist bureaucracy, and in particular its lowest office, the ward, could arbitrate the majority of property disputes between private parties outside the purview of courts, as is further explained in chapter 4.

Thus, the developers operated in a context in which the state owned and actively controlled large portions of HCMC's developable land but also needed their financial participation. The risk of losing investments made in land through expropriation and property disputes started to decrease not through strengthening of legal property rights but through increased information about land development plans and more reasonable compensation.

The New Urban Districts on the Periphery

Another major change in economic conditions occurred when the state increased the supply of developable land. In 1997, the city decided to expand its urban boundary by incorporating 34,670 hectares of land on the periphery into five new urban districts in order to accommodate the city's rapid growth. The city had swollen by an additional one million people during the 1990s and land conversions had already been occurring on the periphery.[3] The annexation of agricultural land meant that the land users in these areas would now be entitled to urban services. The city conducted education programs for the rural population to learn how to use urban facilities. But this annexation also meant that farmers who happened to be living within the new city boundaries would have to eventually relocate to make way for urban development.

The Chief Architect's office set the boundaries of the five new urban districts on the northern, southern, and eastern edges of the city (figure 2.1). Established in major cities by the Prime Minister in 1993 to exercise more control over rapid urbanization, this office wielded significant city planning powers in the beginning of transition (Gainsborough 2005). According to interviews with the head planners in HCMC's Chief Architect's Office, the decisions about new district boundaries were based on population density and whether the majority of the population was already engaged in urban employment.[4] The new District 9 is quite a distance from the city center, however, and many of the wards within it are still primarily rural. Meanwhile, the western portion of the city was not annexed at that time, even though large commercial and residential projects were being developed in areas of the nominally rural Binh Chanh district that were closest to the city center. In fact, one of the most productive firms that I studied, a former state-owned enterprise, was developing 13–80 hectare residential and commercial projects in this area.

Besides increasing the supply of developable land and determining the relocation of the rural population, the designation of the boundaries had important effects on real estate market activities. For example, the land purchasing costs would be lower in non-annexed areas of the periphery; this classification was especially important for large-scale projects such as those occurring in rural district Binh Chanh. While land prices in urban districts were generally higher, they would not appreciate as drastically as when land is converted from agricultural to urban use.

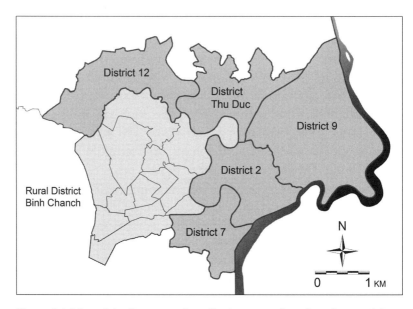

Figure 2.1 Map of the five new urban districts created on the urban periphery of Ho Chi Minh City in 1997 (map is schematic).

Capturing the price differential in land use types was facilitated by the property rights status of agricultural land. The majority of agricultural landholders had been issued their land use certificates, the rough equivalent of land title, as the result of a major drive by the state. These certificates make it a relatively uncomplicated process to sell agricultural land. Meanwhile, the majority of urban parcels did not have the equivalent Building Ownership and Land Use Certificate (BOLUC), which combined housing and urban land tenure certificates into one document pursuant to Decrees 60 and 61, promulgated in July 1994 (DOLA 1998). By 2000 the disparity was significant, with only 5% of urban landholders having received their certificates while 85% of agricultural land holders possessed theirs (Dang and Palmkvist 2001). The distribution of the urban certificates was backlogged for many reasons, including more complicated land tenure clarifications, vagaries in district government capacity to issue them, and tax disincentives for registering (Kim 2004).

In any case, the delay created a situation in which there was a shortage of urban land and housing with clear title, while most agricultural land was fully titled. This gap made it possible to capitalize on the difference if one could find a way to convert agricultural land into urban parcels with title.

The Master Plans

In addition to drawing the city boundaries, the Chief Architect's Office also designed the master plans for the city, determining the location of future residential development and other land uses. Some city planning authority, however, was decentralized to HCMC's 17 urban districts, which were instructed to make their own detailed master plans based on the Chief Architect's more general plan. The districts' detailed plans would indicate specific parcel boundaries where residential uses could be developed as well as the location of future tertiary roads, industrial centers, and other employment areas.

This decentralization was a major restructuring of intergovernmental authority, and it had critical implications for the new market. Districts functioned like bureaucratic fiefdoms in which district leaders could develop their own investment and economic development strategies. Their plans had the powerful effect of determining an agricultural parcel's future potential use and therefore market value. The change would also have dire consequences for farmers because according to regulations, they were supposed to pay a land use change fee of 40% of the land value set by the government, which most could not afford in addition to a 32% income tax for farming (Chinh 1999).

For my case firms, the detailed master plans were one of the primary considerations in choosing project sites. Knowledge about the master plans and the landholdings of public entities such as RESCO are necessary before specific private investment projects can be developed. And yet for much of the early transition period, the plans were formed in secret and were not easily accessible by the general public. While some district offices began to publicly post district master plans, most of these were still being developed and showed only part of their jurisdiction. By 2001, about 60% of the city area had detailed plans at 1:2,000 scale. I collected the available master plans of all five new districts as well as rural districts Binh Chanh in the west and Nha Be in the south. The plans reflect the districts' discretion over land use planning, as they were drawn at different scales ranging from 1:10,000 to 1:2,000 and employed different land use categories.

The uncertainties about the future city plans fueled a speculative real estate market. Firms reported potential windfall gains from insider information and correct guesses about areas slated for residential development and, in particular, areas in close proximity to future roads and highways. Firm #2's leader explained: "Information about government plans is important. The earlier you buy the more profit you make, especially if you buy before the plan is finished. Everything is simple after the master plan is finished and then the price is already high by the time the plan is completed." Obtaining this information is not easy, however, because government bodies themselves will suddenly make changes in their infrastructure development plans.

Rather than implementing additional laws and policies, the state's most effective action in unleashing a firm's private investment was the construction of public works, in particular roads, highways, and bridges. Because the state announces many plans and policies that later are stalled or changed, the firms literally looked for concrete evidence of where public investment actually happens and development will be allowed. Among the firms I studied, this was the most important evidence the firms watched for in order to know when and where to invest in projects themselves. The plethora of legal and policy papers issued by the state had little influence on the firms. Instead of bulwarking legal property rights, the state stabilized the economic landscape and ordered the physical environment with more reasonable compensation rates, master plans, the incorporation of five new districts, and through the location of public infrastructure investments.

Distributing Rights to Develop Urban Land

But the master plans are a bit like the district's wish list. The government does not have enough resources to develop the infrastructure needed to make the periphery urban, and it cannot command private firms to build. While private capital investment was needed, any private firm attempting to obtain the development rights to a specific piece of land had to navigate a maze of government bureaus (see table 3.2). Among these, the key decision-making entities involve three offices. Based on the master plans, the city districts and the Chief Architect's Office coordinate to make the final decision on whether a firm can have development control of a particular site based on the firm's feasibility study. In addition to city and district governments, astonishingly, any development project requesting more than one hectare of land required approval from the Prime Minister's office.

In the beginning of transition, the steps involved in obtaining the various approvals were unclear, and proposals could be delayed for years. The private developers said they were viewed with suspicion and that the likelihood of approval was uncertain. But by the late 1990s, private developers were more accepted and the development process had stabilized. While state entities still enjoy faster approval than private firms, the differences in processing time began to decrease. Furthermore, HCMC started experimenting with expediting the processing of approvals with "one-stop" offices. Generally, all of the firms stated that the business environment had improved significantly and encouraged them to develop land projects, although expedited approvals were still a secondary factor compared to road construction and visible investment in neighboring parcels. Firm #1's leader gave an example: when his firm first bought a land parcel in 1997, project approval cost 300 million VND and lasted an indefinite period of time. By 2000, the fees had halved to 150 million VND ($10,345 USD) and it took 10 months for the project to be approved. These anecdotes confirm the policy literature that emphasizes that decreasing bureaucratic red tape can have a positive effect on the rate of private investment (de Soto 1989; Dowall and Clarke 1991).

However, approval processes became significantly more navigable when decentralization of planning authority increased the importance of the district government.[5] As mentioned earlier, districts could now design the detailed master plan that played a powerful role in determining where development could occur. Furthermore, as can be seen in table 3.2, the district works with other government bodies at the crucial steps 3, 6, and 13, essentially acting as coordinators of urban land development within their jurisdiction. In practice, once the district government approves a project, they can help the proposal gain the other critical approvals.

Therefore, once a district approves a site for use by a particular developer, the property rights of the investor are fairly protected. The district officials in charge of urban development matters said that firms do not compete for land sites so much as apply for sites that have not already been claimed. It was a daily occurrence that investors would come to them to inquire about a site and find that it had already been approved for another project. This is because development right holders cannot sell or transfer their development options for a specific site directly to another private entity; they can sell and transfer the parcels only after they have been developed. Although a firm can share a portion of its project with another firm, the principal applicant must be responsible for developing the proposed project. In fact, a firm's land use right is conditional on their developing the specific proposed project. If they do not begin development within a certain time period, their right reverts to the state. In essence, the government is allocating specific parcels to specific groups in the conversion of land. Once this allocation has been decided, the farmer has no choice but to sell, and he must sell to one particular entity.

In summary, the demographic shifts of rapid urban population and income growth had created such a huge demand for land in HCMC that land transactions were unstoppable and ultimately condoned by the state. The state, however, constrained the supply of developable land through ownership, annexation, land use planning, and the administration of development approval. But they also lacked the finances to develop their own urban development plans. Meanwhile, land use right certificates had been widely distributed to agricultural land on the urban periphery, making it relatively easy to convert into urban land. With scarce supply and high demand for urban land, the potential for profit was great. Still, the pathways to realizing the possibility were unmarked and filled with many challenges. The state had structured a specific institutional framework in which decision making was not transparent and information about specific developable sites was often unavailable. Development authority was decentralized to the sub-city district governments, giving them more discretion in determining the land use of specific sites and a potential role in expediting intergovernmental approvals.

Social Position of the Case Firms

We can now see why social networks and political connections would be important to the work of land development firms. Without open market information and land use planning institutions, information would have to be gathered through private means. It would also be important to gain the support of the district governments in order to obtain investment approval and site control.

Given the importance of private networks, one might think only those who were state elites or related to state elites could become developers in HCMC. One path-dependent hypothesis proposes that political elites would build new economic institutions from previous institutions in such a way that they would become the new capitalist elites. However, in Vietnam, as in many other transition countries, the political cadre did not necessarily benefit during economic transition.[6] Who then was the first generation of private land developers that emerged in HCMC? How did they enter the emerging industry and become real estate entrepreneurs? My fieldwork allowed me to rapidly trace the web of social networks in HCMC's newly emerged real estate market. Spending considerable time living in Vietnam and developing my own networks allowed me to situate the social position of various actors (see appendix). During that time I identified four types of private land development firms operating in HCMC, although one type was not officially registered anywhere (see table 2.1).

The four firm types reflect the background of the entrepreneurs and the evolution of the firm. For example, foreign joint-ventures emerged at the initiative of a foreign entrepreneur wanting to invest in Vietnam. Although the joint-venture would form a Vietnamese-named company and hire Vietnamese staff, the foreign partner in foreign joint-ventures usually played the more active part in project development, with the domestic partner being a state-owned enterprise that contributed land as its share in investment. In the beginning of transition, this arrangement was the only way for foreigners to invest in projects because of the legal restrictions that prohibited granting land use rights to foreigners.

Table 2.1 Typology of private residential real estate development firms in Ho Chi Minh City

Type of Organization	Definition
Investor groups	Flexible groups of part-time developers who hold other full-time jobs but join together to work on a specific project
Professional companies	Organizations with a name, office, and departments with specialized functions and full-time employees
Equitized companies	Former state-owned enterprises that have been permitted to offer private investors stocks and to be managed privately
Foreign joint-ventures	Foreign-owned companies that partner with Vietnamese investors to develop residential projects, among other investment activities

The other three firm types involved domestic entrepreneurs. Some state-owned enterprises were occasionally allowed to "equitize" during different periods of transition (and were sometimes brought back under government ownership again). In the real estate industry, these included state, city, or district construction companies that were allowed to have more autonomy in their operations and possibly take advantage of engaging in more profitable projects. While the state often still owned a controlling share, other citizens, including managers and employees, could become shareholders.

Some new, private real estate companies also started to form. These more typical, professional companies had names, offices, and full-time staff who regularly developed projects. They were different from the investor groups that I also found to be developing significantly sized projects in the urban periphery, although they were not listed anywhere. Investor groups were informal and flexible, in that members might belong to more than one, but each group was focused around the development of a specific project. The majority of a group's members would supply financial capital and occasionally land use rights, while a smaller core who had initiated the group's formation would develop and implement the projects.

There was some correlation between the types of firms and their initial endowment of political capital. Obviously, the equitized companies had the most, as they were still partly state-owned and continued to enjoy special access to land and faster development approvals. Also obvious is that the foreign joint-ventures started with the least, as they were newcomers in a previously closed economy. But the few extraordinarily large land development projects in Vietnam were developed by both the foreign joint-ventures and equitized companies. One might attribute this correlation to their capitalization and economies of scale. Yet this explanation provides only part of the answer, as there were also other firms of these types who could only do few or small projects and were not very successful. In fact, there was little correlation between initial political endowment and the number, size, or success of projects, as we will see in the next chapter.

The fact was that anyone who wanted to become involved with large real estate development projects had to *develop* political connections, because a variety of bureaus controlled access to land development rights and the focus of authority shifted between them over different periods of transition. The relevant issue for analyzing the emergence and success of firms is whether some types of people have better probabilities for developing useful political connections that will privilege their access to land and expedite their approvals. There were some possible characteristics that were not factors in determining who became an entrepreneur. These include attributes that Vietnamese might refer to in other contexts to situate people, such as sharing the same hometown, alma mater, military experience, and Communist Party membership. The people who worked together on projects varied in these respects.

There are certainly those for whom it would be highly unlikely to develop fruitful relationships with local government. For example, those with problematic political histories are discriminated against in educational and employment opportunities. But I did find that state actors were willing to form new working relationships increasing the pool of participants in the new market. This is in contrast to what happened in Hanoi, which will be discussed in chapter 6.

There were a few things the entrepreneurs in HCMC did have in common. They were all educated males, ranging in age from their 30s to their early 50s. These attributes imply that the entrepreneurs did not possess special knowledge about real estate development at the beginning of transition. Had they been older, they might have been able to draw on earlier market experience gained before Vietnam's Communist revolution. Many firms had key members who were or had been professors in the fields of economics or business, but of course they had not been trained in market economics when they received their advanced degrees in one of the Soviet Union countries. The firms often recruited key members who had had some type of previous construction experience, either in a state-owned company or an engineering occupation.

This demographic does fit with other studies of entrepreneurs in transition countries in eastern Europe and China. The younger population and those with cultural capital fared relatively better in the transition to a market economy than did the older and rural population. Eyal, Szelenyi, and Townsley (1998) found in their surveys of firms in Poland, Hungary, and the Czech Republic that a narrow political economy hypothesis does not hold. Specifically, those who had political capital and no cultural capital during the transition lost privilege and power, although those who had both were often the biggest winners. They attribute this distinction to the unique political context of Central Europe, where those who managed the transition came from an alliance of the new politocracy and opinion-making intellectual elites who promoted civil society and economic rationalism. In the new technocratic system, cultural capital became more valuable than political capital generated from old positions in the Communist Party or bureaucracy (Eyal, Szelenyi, and Townsley 1998).

Although the Asian transition did not undergo such major political reforms, we also find that political capital seems to generate declining returns as transition progresses and does not predict well who becomes and succeeds as an entrepreneur (Nee 1989, 1996). Whether we can attribute this shift to the nature of market economies themselves, this study cannot pursue. The framing of a duality between political and cultural capital seems overly drawn, however. In China as well as in Vietnam, political elites did amass private wealth, including land. But in my investigation, entrepreneurial firms consisted of members with both types of capital. The key was for those with either to find one another and form relations through new social networks. Because the economic environment was so challenging but the potential for profit so great, people who wanted to pursue land development projects needed and desired the cooperation of others.

Stark (2001) makes the point that the shape of a firm's networks depends on the development and availability of networks before the transition. For example, in his comparisons of the links of cross-ownership and investment in industrial firms in Hungary and the Czech Republic, he found that Hungarian firms after the transition were heavily networked directly with one another, which was a logical progression from the relationships enterprises had already developed with during the 1970s, when Hungary's brand of socialism loosened. Meanwhile, in the Czech Republic, firms might have links to the same banks and investment funds but no direct ownership ties with one another. Stark argues that this different structure of firm networks mirrors the lower degree of autonomy that Czech enterprises had to form relationships with one another during the Communist era and the relationships they were allowed to develop with industry and regional associations, which continue to be resilient in the post-Communist period (Stark 2001).

Stark's work focuses on the strategies of the managers of state-owned factories, whom he paints as risk-averse and coping with an uncertain environment. In the case of real estate in Vietnam, however, the development of new firms in a new industry required new networks. But perhaps HCMC did have an institutional inheritance that contributed to the formation of new networks that assisted the emergence and operations of firms. Even before the official *doi moi* reforms in 1986, Vietnam area specialists note that for pragmatic reasons, local governments and citizens could not and did not observe the central government's economic plans very closely but practiced considerable discretion in implementing them (Fforde and de Vylder 1996). Some characterize HCMC's government as especially cooperative with private business (Dapice et al. 2004). But others take issue with the characterization of HCMC as an exceptional reformer within the country, since its government elites siphon off state assets and practice gatekeeping as often as in other parts of the country (Gainsborough 2003).

In any case, I found that in HCMC social networks were amazingly open to new entrants and to new connections between existing networks. This egalitarian hypersociability certainly made it easier for me to do my research. People were chatty. They would talk to me and to my young assistants and to other people ranging widely in age, occupation, and social standing with an attitude of possibility. In my research and everyday transactions, I observed that people generally tried to work with one another, or could be persuaded to do so. It would be a rare occurrence that negotiation would stop altogether.

In this milieu of social networking, the entrepreneurs recounted to me their personal histories of how they came to be real estate entrepreneurs which indicated a blend of happenstances and structured privilege. An entrepreneur might mention knowing a ward official because of his status as a war hero, studying abroad, taking over a father's business, and so forth. But they would also usually tell stories of how they fell into real estate by tagging along with a friend on their first project. The point is that there were a variety of paths. One's initial endowment of networks and political connections were not determining factors. Rather, networks needed to be developed. And in HCMC, the development of networks and connections were facilitated by its culture, but were especially accessible to educated, sociable, younger adult males. The most convincing indicator of the open entry into the market is that hundreds of new firms formed. We will see in chapter 6 that this openness was not available in other parts of the country, where almost no private firms formed, and that one of the major differences between the regions is the openness of the social networks.

This chapter has described how large demographic shifts created a demand for urban land. The significant constraints on its supply by the state's land administration pushed potential profit levels for land conversion on the urban periphery even higher. But realizing the potential gain would be difficult for any would-be private entrepreneurs. This chapter suggests that HCMC's sociability helped individuals to build the social networks and political connections needed to work in a challenging economic environment in which information was limited and not transparent, to navigate the bureaucratic maze, and to make development projects happen. The next chapter will explain in greater detail how my case firms found ways to work within the structural constraints and which ones were successful.

Notes

1. These sales are not exactly informal land transactions in that the formalities, rather than being ignored, had not yet been defined. HCMC's real estate market is not best characterized as a dual formal and informal market. Rather, transactions exhibit a spectrum of official condoning through the stamp witness of ward governments, tax receipts, and building permits (Kim 2004).

2. The term is 20–50 years for agricultural land and 90 years for diplomatic land (*Law on Land* 2003).

3. Population figures for HCMC have been controversial because estimates have varied widely. For 2000, they range from conservative official figures of 5 million to estimates of over 7 million. As was the case in centrally planned economies, it is undesirable to have statistics that do not reflect policy targets. Yet it is also a difficult task to count unregistered migrants who have flooded the cities looking for jobs. One key informant, who helped implement the Statistical Office of HCMC's official census in 1999, claimed meticulous procedures, even counting homeless people on the streets. Whatever the total number, the official statistics state that HCMC added over a million people to its population in a decade. The Statistical Office of HCMC recorded a total population figure for the greater HCMC area of 3.64 million in 1989, increasing to 4.77 million in 1999. This growth was not even throughout the city, however. For the inner urban district areas, population grew by 21% during those 10 years. In the five new urban districts on the edge of HCMC, the Statistical Office counted an even more rapid population growth of 58% (485,965 to 768,236 people) and in the rural districts on the fringe of the city an increase of 73% (358,833 to 620,888) (HCMC Statistical Yearbook 2000). These statistics indicate high levels of land development pressure in HCMC's urban periphery.

4. Interview with Deputy Chief Architect Dr. Eng. Vo Kim Cuong, June 11, 2001.

5. As we will see in the next chapter, some firms were able to bypass the district government and work directly with the city and national governments.

6. In the former Soviet Union transition countries, policy advisors feared that if the politically powerful did not gain economically, the historic transition would reverse and the communist party would regain power. In order to ensure lasting transition, shock-therapy policy advice tried to destroy the old government institutions and import ones that might transform the incentives of people (Sachs 1995; Roland 2000).

3

Who Succeeds as an Entrepreneur in Ho Chi Minh City

This chapter presents how the first generation of entrepreneurs practically went about developing their investment projects in a difficult economic environment. This analysis is core to the transition puzzle, because with a lack of market data, a shortage of formal financing, unclear bureaucratic procedures and policies, and an interventionist state, most conventional policy experts thought that it would be impossible for entrepreneurs to regularly develop large investment projects. It is also puzzling because these entrepreneurs were able to engage in novel economic activities when they did not necessarily have powerful positions in society before the transition. How did they do it?

Because there are so many competing theories about why people change their economic behavior, I focus on a narrow unit of observation. I examine the new entrepreneurs' key new economic acts. These include the four critical steps involved with developing urban land in the periphery of HCMC: 1) finding land for potential project sites; 2) negotiating a compensation price with the current users, usually farmers; 3) assembling development capital; and 4) processing the many permits and approvals needed to implement the project. As I explained in the previous chapter, the state structured many aspects of these steps.

In exploring how the entrepreneurs were able to develop their projects, I did not look for answers in general but in specific. Of the 200 or so firms that were operating in HCMC at the time of the study, I developed detailed case studies of fourteen of them (table 3.1) and determined how each one actually implemented each phase of its projects, step by step.[1]

These grounded, empirical findings lead to surprising observations. We find that in order to understand how the new

Table 3.1   The fourteen case firms in Ho Chi Minh City, 2001

Firm type	Firm #	Projects	Land area	Total units	Product type
Investor group	1	1	3	20	serviced lots
	2	4	5.2	109	serviced lots
	3	2	50	1060	serviced lots, foundation
Professional company	4	3	0	75	villas
	5	5	40	1852	serviced lots, houses
	6	3	14.7	279	serviced lots
	7	3	44	568	serviced lots, villas
	8	4	19	1002	serviced lots
	N1	6	—	—	serviced lots, houses
Equitized company	9	1	243.5	2938	serviced lots, houses, resettlement areas
	10	—	—	600	houses
Foreign investor company	11	7	13.82	1279	houses, villas, apartments, serviced lots
	12	2	5.7	46	villas
	N2	2	8	—	—

Note. Projects: number of projects completed or under construction. Land area is given in hectares. Units are developed land parcels or housing units, depending on project type.

entrepreneurs engage in these new acts, particularly the most successful firms, cognitive processes are fundamental. That is, they had to learn many things and, in particular, new ways of thinking. Furthermore, their learning process was highly social. The importance of social networks discussed in the last chapter is about more than the instrumental tidbits of market information that are passed through them; it is about the spread of the Vietnamese market paradigm.

As we start investigating the changes in individuals we see that society has shaped their cognition and that agents must share cognitive frameworks for real institutional change to occur. The following two chapters will discuss how institutional change is social and cognitive.

The Importance of Institutional Arrangements and Intermediaries

Finding Available Land

The first of the four key steps in pursuing an urban land development project in HCMC involves finding a potential project site. The firms I studied focused on the urban periphery for several reasons. First, agricultural land is much cheaper than urban land, and larger parcels are available and more easily consolidated. Larger projects can achieve lower development costs through economies of scale. Furthermore, because the urban periphery is not as built up as the city center, compensation negotiations involve fewer households. Still, within the 44,000 hectares surrounding HCMC, the firms must decide where and how much land they will attempt to obtain. These decisions are crucial since location provides the bulk of any housing project's market value.

In order to determine the location and amount of land they would develop, developers required three kinds of information. They needed market information about where land would appreciate rapidly in value. They also needed to know where the district would allow them to develop projects, per the detailed master plans they were designing. And finally, they had to obtain information about current land users and neighbors in order to gauge compensation costs and expropriation risks. As Firm #2 put it, "Information is the most key. Misleading information is dangerous." As I studied how firms approached finding land, I found that they used a variety of social networks and institutional arrangements to obtain different kinds of information and to arrive at a decision about which land parcels they would attempt to develop.

Nearly all of the firms collected some information about real estate market trends, but their data varied in quality.[2] Because there are no sources for comprehensive price data in the city, some of the firms made general observations about demographic trends such as population growth, density, and job growth. Some compared average land price estimates between districts. These price estimates were anecdotal, and since districts are large areas with high price variation within them, they were limited in their usefulness in identifying specific parcels. The more savvy firms tried to gauge price trends in a more systematic fashion. Firm #4 gathered price data about wards and streets through enquiries with local landbrokers, visits to property exchange centers where real estate listings are posted, and tracking listings in the real estate sections of local newspapers.

Landbrokers could be a significant source of market data in HCMC during the transition. I conducted a survey of 774 landbrokers in 2000 and found that almost every one of the 250 wards in my study area had at least a few landbrokers who specialize in selling land in their ward, although their levels of expertise varied. In the agricultural periphery, impromptu landbrokers abound, advertising with signs on the side of main roads. Landbrokers can range from a street snack-seller who can also sell you a house to established offices that have been brokering deals for 15 years and have support staff. Furthermore, since landbrokers do not represent a profession with rigorous standards, the reliability of their information and their scruples in brokering deals can vary considerably. But they also face risks; one landbroker complained bitterly to me of not being paid her commission for Firm #3's first project. A landbroker's knowledge is also spatially limited to the one or few wards in which they have a history of sales data.

As a result of the risks in dealing with landbrokers, brick-and-mortar property centers, as well as Internet property centers, began to emerge. Most of the centers, although offering no assurances, also help verify ownership of sites. Firms #4, #5, and #6 decided to form their own property exchange centers in order to make their companies greater hubs for real estate transactions, bring in potential customers for their own projects, improve name recognition, and gain additional information about market demand.

Some of the firms formalized the market analysis function into their organization. Firm #11 had a full-time employee whose sole job was to collect market information. This firm also collected their own housing demand data by conducting formal surveys of shoppers who had come into their offices inquiring about properties, including those who decided not to purchase one of their units. The recently equitized Firm #10 conducted an annual study of market demand. They categorized customers into three groups (high income, average income, and low income), and they presented different hypothetical housing products to them in order to appraise demand for housing types (rowhouses, villas, and apartments) and features (interior decoration options, feng shui, size, location, and price).

In addition to market data, the firms needed information about which land parcels the government would allow them, a private company, to develop. My case firms confirmed that the districts' master plans were one of the largest considerations in choosing project sites. Knowledge about the master plans and the landholdings of RESCO, the city's real estate conglomerate, is necessary before specific sites can be considered. And yet for much of the transition period, these plans were formed in secret and not easily accessible to the general public in some districts. The firms had to find ways to access this information or at least ways to improve the probability that they choose sites that the district would approve.

I found that the equitized companies and Firm #6, which originally started in Hanoi, were quite secretive about the way they found land sites. They refused to explain how they found land except to say that it was a combination of the master plan and market demand. But they did state that they preferred not to use landbrokers. Firm #6 said that "information can be leaked, and secrecy and information are worth a lot in this business. You want to buy before other people know." Instead, they hired their own staff of landbrokers, "people who were born to do real estate." They contracted three or four people to work within a district to help them find land. In addition, the staff in their department of projects had developed relationships with bureaucrats in the districts in which they worked, who often supply leads about land available for large projects.

Firms also hired consulting companies to locate properties. Real estate consulting companies are usually private-like businesses of a larger state-owned enterprise that will help locate land, process permits faster, and do urban design work. In Vietnam, consulting companies have emerged in a variety of sectors to help expedite business transactions. In effect, they sell their political connections to firms. One company helped both Firms #1 and #3 to find parcels in the district that had hired them to draw the master plan. Because of their involvement with the master plan, they had inside information about which parcels would most likely be located near future public investments and where their other politically well-connected clients were developing projects. They presented several options for Firm #3's large project. Firm #11 hired a state-owned consulting company to gather information from the district about the number of people living in their project areas in order to assess compensation rates.

Another surprising source of information for the firms is other firms. Because the state plays such a large role in land allocation, there was little fierce competition between firms over land sites. Most of the professional firms I studied listed five or six companies with whom they are in regular contact. In this cooperative business environment, there has even been talk of forming a real estate industry association. RESCO initiated a meeting in April 2000 with the support of the local government offices to ask private companies to establish a real estate association with RESCO as the head. The aim would be to ensure that competing companies obey the law and share information. The proposed benefits of such an association were accountability for builders to adhere to construction quality standards and the ability to coordinate companies that were competing in the same area and driving up land compensation prices. Not surprisingly, the firms I spoke to said they were wary of joining a government-led industry association.

After assessing market demand information about general areas and information about the district's master plan, private as well as public land developers start to home in on specific parcels and investigate the identity of the current owners as well as the owners of neighboring parcels. They also try to assess which parcels might be relatively easy to obtain. Land negotiations with and compensation of farmers are by far the most difficult step for all developers, an issue that I discuss in the next section. Therefore, all of the firms try to minimize the difficulty by attempting to assess at the outset how likely it is that the current use right owner will sell them the right without complications. Or in the words of Firm #6, they try to buy land cheaply from those who are broke.

In addition, all of the firms are trying to find out information about the identity of the owners of the neighboring land parcels. Locating near a politically powerful owner helps them hedge against the risk of property expropriation and unexpected public works. For example, Firms #1 and #2 bought parcels next to a site that was purchased by members of Petrolimex, a state-owned oil exporting company (see figure 3.1). Also, firms take cues about potential land values by observing the land investment activities of neighbors. And some will try to locate near recently developed or transacted parcels in order to minimize their infrastructure development costs.

Uncovering information about the political importance and financial status of landowners, let alone their identity, is challenging, especially in the face of outdated cadastral records that have not been able to keep up with the rapid growth in land transactions. Rather, this type of information requires detailed, local knowledge through an intermediary. Firms most commonly engaged local private landbrokers and ward officers who live in the neighborhood and know the people personally.

Landbrokers and ward officers obtain information through an inherently social process. A veteran and highly successful landbroker in District 9 who introduced parcels to Firms #1 and #3 described it as the outflow of a shared history through alma maters, military service, neighborhood associations, parties, anniversaries, and memorial services that bring people together. This landbroker could also regularly get information about master plan formation through her friendships with local ward officers and the wives of district officials. However, some firms avoided using landbrokers or used them only occasionally because they found them unreliable. For example, developers recounted instances where landbrokers lied to them about sales prices and pocketed the difference. Meanwhile, one landbroker reported that she is much more likely to work with someone who has been sent to her by referral. She avoids strangers because they may be dishonest: "So many VIPs are broke these days." She will visit the investors at their houses to make sure she knows where

| Firm #1 1997 Investor group of 20 2 hectares | Petrolimex SOE 1993 8 SJC 4 hectares | 1995 Investor group of 10 4 hectares |
| | | Firm #2 1998 Investor group of 15 people 4 hectares |

Figure 3.1 Diagram of progression of parcels purchased by case firms.

they live. For example, she was willing to help the leader of Firm #1 because she is good friends with his brother-in-law.

Ward officers also utilized information flows through social networks. The ward officer who helped broker land in District 12 to Firm #1 explained, "This area is the countryside, there are not many people so people get to know one another—you go to one another's weddings, anniversaries, and memorial services." Ward officers have some additional advantages over landbrokers. Firm #4 said, "Wards are more important because they are closer to those who own the land. They act like consultants. People in the ward coordinate with the Department of Land and Housing people to draw boundaries on each parcel, getting land owner-ship information."

What becomes clear from observing each of the firms' strate-gies in locating developable sites is that they needed the help of intermediaries. Some of these were for hire such as the consulting companies and landbrokers. But the knowledge of the need for intermediaries and which ones to access came through a social networking process. The head of Firm #1, a professor, happened to attend a training program with the head of a consulting com-pany that later helped him with his projects. He also took me around to visit his friends in three different district offices. Firm #2 had friends who referred them to local landbrokers. Firm #3 had friends in District 9's government before it started its project. Firm #4 had personal friendships with ward officers. Firm #8's director's friends told him that the land in District 7 near Firm #11's projects would be valuable. As discussed earlier, social net-works were open and kept expanding. The key for firms was to find links that reached the politically connected and those who had useful information. In this way, those who might not be politically well connected themselves could make friends or find intermediaries to connect to them.

The spatial location of their social networks bounded the firms' land information and therefore their project site consid-erations. In particular, the investor groups, Firms #1 and #3, and to a lesser extent Firm #2, restricted themselves to specific wards within one district. What is interesting is that it was not their political connections that determined their ability to consider a wider market. Firm #3 has very strong political connections, but it chose to stay in one area. In contrast, the politically well-connected equitized Firms #10 and #11 and the professional Firm #5 developed projects in a wide variety of locations. But for firms #10 and #5 the geographical diversity was a result of their ability to form new relationships. Firm #5 used landbrokers they had never met before. The large Firm #10 developed new working relationships with local ward officers. Its staff would send letters to wards for appointments and get to know the chairmen of the ward and the officers in charge of land administration.

As for deciding the amount of land to buy once a location had been determined, the firms cited a variety of factors. Capital constraints were balanced by the benefits of economies of scale. Firm #6 explains that if it bought only half the amount of land for its projects, developing infrastructure would be difficult. They can spread these large expenses over more units if they have a larger parcel. State regulations also affected how much land they bought. Firm #5 said it was difficult to do projects larger than two hectares because the city and district governments wanted the private firms to develop only relatively small projects.

In summary, in the absence of updated, publicly accessible land use plans, land registration records, industry reports, and comprehensive market studies, reliable information is difficult to obtain. So the firms synthesize information gathered through a variety of institutional arrangements accessed through social relationships. The classes of information that are most influential in their decision about where to locate their projects are the district's master plans, market values, a parcel's proximity to road and highway investments, the political power of neighboring parcel owners, and the economic status of the current landholder. The firm's members' preexisting political connections were helpful, but they did not determine a firm's ability to locate land. Rather, it was their ability to develop and expand social and working relationships to access the various sources of local knowledge. Developing these relationships takes time and talent. If firms did not use networks and establish institutional

arrangements for finding project sites, they would spend inordi-
nate amounts of time looking for land and face considerable risk
about the reliability of the information they were getting, to the
point of rendering themselves unproductive.

Land Compensation Negotiations

Once a site has been selected, firms need to buy the land use
rights. When they buy land, they incur two kinds of expense:
compensation to the current user and money to the government, the official owner, in the form of a land use right fee.
Compensation negotiations are the most important and difficult
step in developing a project, in large part determining its feasibility and profitability. This section, then, will analyze the process of negotiating a sales price.

In the early years of transition, development firms had the
upper hand in negotiations with farmers. If the project fit the
master plan and had been approved, the government bodies
generally helped the developer transfer the land use right from
the current user. Farmers were sometimes railroaded into settling for low prices. The growing social tension about this practice began to erode the legitimacy of the state, changing the
parameters for the negotiation. The institutional environment is
now structured such that individual farmers can delay projects
by refusing to agree to a proposed price.

Once the parties agree on a price, the formal process involves
the farmer officially releasing his land back to the state while
the buyer simultaneously applies to the state for the right to use
the land. Reaching an agreement, however, can be challenging.
Land compensation is especially arduous for larger projects that
require the assembly of many parcels. For example, Firms #3's
large project site of 25 hectares required buying land from 30
farmers. Trying to buy parcels from multiple owners has well-
known difficulties. The last ones to sell can negotiate higher
prices than the initial sellers because the developer is fairly close
to realizing the project. But when the previous sellers find out
about the new higher sales prices, they often want to renegotiate

the sale they already made. I found that the firms I studied handled the negotiations in a wide variety of ways in terms of who in the firm negotiated, whether outside parties assisted, and the terms of the agreement.

In the case of the investor groups, the leaders themselves negotiated with the farmers, largely because they were the only ones in the group developing the projects. In addition, Firm #8's leader also represented his firm because it is a relatively small organization with only two departments to handle sales and accounting. All of the other firms had departments, usually called some variation of "the Project Department," whose main function was to settle land compensation negotiations. Settling compensation is a step in the land development process that requires significant investment in labor. For example, the relatively small Firm #7 had a separate Compensation Department staffed by three of their 14 employees. Firm #9 employed 10 people in their Department of Negotiation who dealt full-time with compensation and relocation. These staff members meet with farmers and try to convince them to relocate at a low price.

Nearly all of the firms used the assistance of intermediaries in their negotiations with farmers. But there was variation in who these intermediaries were that seemed to correlate with the size of the firm. In the smaller firms, such as Firms #1, #2, and #8, and also in Firm #10's smaller projects, members would talk directly with individual farmers in meetings overseen by landbrokers and ward officials. Landbrokers typically earn 1–3% of the sale price. As mentioned earlier, landbrokers were often the ones assisting the developers in discerning who might be willing to sell land easily when they were considering parcels at the outset.

Ward officials are usually the witnesses to land transaction contracts, including informal transactions that can be formalized later. Firms with smaller projects tended to have fewer difficulties in the negotiations. In one case, the leader of Firm #1 took me to visit one of the farmers he bought land from, whom he allows to remain on the site until he is ready to build. Firm #2 also usually had a relatively easy time with negotiations. For one of their projects in District 9, the firm completed direct negotiations with four farmers in two meetings. Basically, the farmers made an offer and the firm accepted it. The firm leader explained that it was easy because the farmers did not need the land for their farming and wanted to stop farming eventually anyway. Another effective technique in completing negotiations for these smaller projects was to compensate the farmers in cash immediately. Firms #1, #2, and #8 stated that they bring the total amount in gold to the farmer's house at the final meeting.

Ward officials often serve as more than witnesses. Sometimes they broker the transaction and receive a commission. In the case of Firm #7, firm representatives are not present at the negotiations; rather, it enlists the ward officers to negotiate on its behalf. Its project department team members attend only the final transaction. Firm #4 keeps its identity secret because it "can't relocate people who know," and it also uses the wards and district officers to negotiate on its behalf. The farmers are at a disadvantage in these cases, not knowing the identity of the buyer or their ability to pay. Government officers negotiating with farmers will typically refer to the state "frame" prices printed in land valuation tables, which are significantly below market prices. Firm #7 says that negotiators usually argue that the price is reasonable compared to what the farmers have invested so far, that the farmer's land has to urbanize eventually according to the master plan, and that the state frame price is the regulated price.

Some firms, however, bypassed the ward officers and approached district government officers to help in the negotiations. While the ward officers have the most detailed knowledge about individual households and parcels, they have little decision-making power, and some firms viewed them as not worth dealing with. On the other hand, the district level of government has a great deal of discretionary power in making land use decisions, since it determines the district master plan and approves individual projects. Firms need political weight to be able to directly access the districts. For example, one of the leaders spearheading investor group Firm #3 was the chair of HCMC's Workers' Union in addition to being a professor at the Technical University. The unions are part of the Communist Party and are organized hierarchically; they have their own funds and can exert influence on the central government in Hanoi as well as the university. Firm #3 had difficulty in negotiating its first project, which involved purchasing land from more than 30 different farmers, all of whom had their land certificates. When some did not want to sell or asked too high a price, this investor group enlisted the help of district officials to persuade the farmers that it would be a win-win situation and that they must sell at the state-regulated price. The compensation negotiations concluded in six months, and the farmers vacated immediately after the sale. About ten of the parcels in the project were bought by district officials. Similarly, Firm #9 is the district's real estate company, which equitized in 1999 from RESCO. Therefore, they have very close relations with the district where they have been able to clear hundreds of hectares of land.

In addition to district officials, the equitized companies also took advantage of their ability to engage the help of civil unions and associations such as the Women's Association, the Youth Union, the Retired People's Association, and so forth, to also try to persuade and put peer pressure on farmers to sell. Firm #10 explained: "These groups are closer to the people and they explain the government's policies to farmers and convince them. Farmers belong to these groups already. Farmers do not trust ward and district officers, assuming they are doing under-the-table deals with investors." These firms elicit the help of the ward officers, who know the leaders of each association, to engage them in the negotiation effort. This seems to fit with the social norm I observed during my time in Vietnam, where economic disputes are not the domain of just the buyers and sellers but often a community event. For example, in minor traffic accidents, a group will quickly form around the parties and have a discussion to decide who is at fault and who should pay whom and the amount. People not directly involved still feel entitled to give their input in shaping settlements.

Large foreign joint-venture investors bypassed much of this trouble once they gained approval for their projects from the city and national government, because relocating and compensating the current occupants then became the city and district's responsibility. This arrangement is necessary because a foreigner would have no legitimacy in moving people off the land. For example, it took Firm #11 nearly a decade of relationship building with the city and central government and a number of infrastructure development projects before it was approved for development rights to 2,600 hectares on the southern edge of HCMC. Of this area, 600 hectares have been cleared so far, and the firm has built or planned projects in about 490 of these hectares. The compensation money is given from the firm to the state-owned consulting company that handles the negotiations with the farmers. That this firm does not have to deal with compensation in their project area is a big selling point in attracting investors. Firm #11's project service department's supervisor explained: "It's a big risk for investors. They can't find anywhere else in Vietnam like us. Prices might seem very low in other places, but you just don't know about compensation."

The length of negotiations varied simply by size of project. Firms #1, #2, #6, and #8 typically took about one month to complete negotiations for their projects that were about one hectare in size. The larger projects of Firms #3, #7, #8, #9, and #12 took about six months to two years, depending on the size of the project and how difficult the negotiations were. But in a project of any size, negotiations could reach an impasse, stalling the project indefinitely. For example, for Firm #2's project in the Thu Duc district, it had already paid 50% of the agreed price for land but the project had been stalled for three years.

Even after an initial agreement, firms reported instances of difficulty making agreed prices stick. A member of Firm #6 recounted his experience as a vice-director of another real estate company that was developing a residential project in Thu Duc District. To complete land assembly the firm had to negotiate with only two more farmers, but the agreed price kept changing when the firm would return to deliver the payment. At first they agreed on 300,000 VND/sqm. Two days later, the price became 500,000 VND/sqm, which they renegotiated down to 470,000. But then five days later the price rose to 750,000 VND/sqm, even though these farmers did not have land use certificates. As I will discuss further in the next chapter, the information and power asymmetries in the negotiation between farmers and firms led to pushback from society and the central government. Thus, farmers exercised greater ability not to agree to a compensation price. Firms found three ways of coping with intransigent sellers. Sometimes they offered more compensation. For example, Firm #6 said that since the introduction of policy reforms which limited the district government's participation in land compensation negotiations, if a farmer refuses to sell, the firm will offer a price above the market rate.

Another method of coping with an impasse in negotiations has been to reduce project size if enough of the project site has been secured. For example, Firm #7 states that although it has not had to completely cancel any of its projects so far, it has had to reduce the size of one project from ten hectares to three hectares. Firm #8 said it also reduces project size if it cannot negotiate a lower price. A third technique, which reduces the project size less drastically, is to offer developed land units as a form of compensation to the farmers.

Officially, a firm should complete the stages 1–17 in table 3.2 and gain investment approval before attempting to buy land. But the project approval process takes time, and the land assembly and compensation negotiations themselves can take six months to two years. The market land price and therefore the compensation prices could rise drastically if the firms waited. As a result, some firms begin buying land unofficially as they begin the project approval process.

In summary, compensating farmers for the land they occupy is one of the most important issues in Vietnam. The methods that these firms have used to deal with this difficult step in the land development process is to be secretive about their identity, to use intermediaries, and use government representatives and social institutions to put pressure on the farmers to sell. This step in the development process is obviously a highly political one. The next chapter discusses the relative power dynamics. For our purposes here, we observed how the entrepreneurs, especially those working on larger projects, needed the active help of different state and nonstate actors in order to complete the negotiations, the most critical step of developing urban land projects.

Financing Projects

As the firms find sites to develop and negotiate with farmers for the transfer of land use rights, they need financing to pay for the land compensation and construction. Development costs varied considerably between firms and projects, depending in part on whether the developer was planning to build a luxurious villa subdivision at $450 per square meter or plots of land serviced by basic infrastructure at $28 per square meter. Most firms' projects were of the latter type, however, and they estimated that 30–50% of the project budget was devoted to costs related to purchasing the land use rights. The significance of this portion, the variability of the expense, and the early timing help explain why the firms negotiate so hard with the farmers and why they seek cheap land on the periphery of the city. Another 50–60% of the budget was used for physical infrastructure development of the land. The firms used a variety of strategies to reduce their construction costs. Some integrated the construction function into their firm in order to lower their costs and have better construction management. With the huge population migration from the countryside to the city, no firm ever reported any difficulty in contracting construction labor, or any shortages of construction materials. Several firms, however, did cite the shortage of development capital financing as an impediment in their operations.

One institutional arrangement that all of the firms used for development financing was to have customers make installment payments as the project developed. For example, Firm #9 collected deposits from 151 households before they began construction of their project in Binh Hung ward. The earlier a customer is willing to buy into a project, the lower the sales price of the unit and the better the location of their unit. In general, buyers pay 30% as a down payment and make another one or two installments at different stages of the project's completion. The industry standard is for the customers to pay the last 10–20% of the purchase price after they receive their formal land use right certificate. Customers said they like this option because they can spread out the payments without incurring financing costs or putting up the collateral required for the newly emerging but still expensive bank mortgages. They can collect savings from their extended families. The willingness on the part of households to pay installments before construction is high enough to make this collection method a regular financing strategy. Private firms are able to access private household savings, which have grown with HCMC's rising incomes, in a way that the state has not been able to do.

Regardless of high demand, selling products before they are completed also requires the firms to invest in sales and marketing to ensure a regular flow of customers who will find and buy a particular firm's product rather than other options. Eight of the firms studied advertised their projects in the real estate section of newspapers and Internet listings. Six of them also rented space in property exchange centers or set up their own in their offices, where they created large displays explaining the location, the plan of subdivided lots, information about the project, and contact information. Eight of the firms had a separate sales or marketing department and employed full-time sales agents. These energetic people would call potential customers and meet them to take them to see the development site. One sales agent said that one competitive advantage the firm tries to use is exceptional service. For example, some potential customers are so busy that she will come to their house with maps and documents and escort them to the site if they are interested. She finds potential customers through her own social network.

In order to access household savings, the firms must develop a good reputation. Through social networking, buyers bring other buyers to join the project. In fact, this was the only source of financing for the investor group Firms #1, #2, and #3. The networks of friends and associates who joined into the project through word of mouth were so widespread that people only loosely knew one another. These associations are remarkable in light of the large size of Firm #3's projects, which had more than 500 units. As the firms target customers beyond their social network, they invest more of their labor and capital in marketing and sales. Firm #11 had a sales office much like the type used in Taiwan. When a potential customer enters the sales office, a row of young women in uniforms stands up together, bowing and belting out greetings in unison. This practice is especially curious since Vietnamese do not bow to one another. Inside the luxurious sales center are model displays of their projects, a lounge area with drinks, a wall of little red certificates with names of customers who have bought into the projects, and life-size model rooms illustrating how the interiors of the units can be furnished. There are also large wall displays showing the long-term development plans approved by HCMC's People's Committee for this area of the city. The sales agents can also escort visitors to see model homes. Likewise, the small joint-venture Firm #12 set up a model home and full-time sales agents in a fashion similar to those used in the United States.

But the customers bear most of the development risk in this financing arrangement. I had to abandon one of the firms I initially studied, N1, when its leader was imprisoned in November 2001 for collecting 11.5 billion VND ($793,000 USD) from 289 workers in a tobacco company but failing to deliver the units. One of the former partners of the firm, who is now special assistant to the head of Firm #4, told me that Firm N1 overleveraged the company's capital and used the development capital from one project to help pay for other projects. While this firm had built up its name recognition, it started too many projects at once and had to keep starting new projects and collect installment payments to finance projects already begun. Eventually, the firm could not deliver units, leading to scandal and the incarceration of the firm's leaders. Firm #10's marketing manager said, "What's important is good reputation. The price must be competitive but also delivering the land certificate is important. If it takes 5–6 years to obtain it, that's a bad reputation. If it takes 1–5 years, you have a good reputation."

Another source of financing for all of the firms except the investor groups involved offering shares of the company to investors. One key informant cited cases where investors contributed land to the project and received 60% of the developed units as their dividend. As in the case of compensating farmers, land itself has increasingly become the currency of transactions in the face of capital constraints. Usually shareholders invest cash, however. For Firm #9, 35% of the shares were owned by local government and 65% were held by company managers and employees. The shares did so well that the firm was able to offer a 24% after-tax dividend in 2000 and 40% in 2001. For recently equitized Firm #10, 40% of the shares were owned by local government, 20% by their own workers and managers, and 40% by private individuals and state-owned enterprises. Firm #6's shareholders included individuals and private and state-owned banks. Firm #12, a small joint-stock firm, openly showed the identity of shareholders in a display at their sales office. Firm #5 listed nine individuals with different percentages of ownership in an internal document intended to explain the firm to potential investors. In both cases, however, I later found ghost owners behind the publicized names and faces.

Another strategy that some of the firms use to finance projects is to reinvest profits from previous projects. Firms commonly split larger projects into phases, and once the cash flow from one phase is sufficient, they can begin the next phase. Firm #4, which had a 30% profit margin on high-priced projects and a 15–20% profit margin on low-priced ones, reinvested about half the profit into new projects. Firms #5 and #11 were able to do this as a regular practice. Firm #9 even made enough profit to cross-subsidize an affordable housing project.[3] As mentioned earlier, however, some firms have run into trouble by overextending themselves.

Another method of closing the gap in development capital is to collaborate with other firms. RESCO, the large city-owned real estate company, as well as some of its equitized companies, will offer smaller portions of its large development project to the professional real estate companies. Although state-owned companies have advantages in gaining control of sites and approvals, the private companies generally have better access to private capital and are more nimble and efficient in developing projects. In addition, firms may sometimes coordinate their projects to share infrastructure costs. For example, Firm #6 showed me maps that illustrated how collaboration with another firm's project to share infrastructure lines had shaped its project's boundaries.

A few of the firms did finance a portion of their projects with bank loans. This was the most expensive option, however, and they tried to use it as little as possible. In addition, loans cannot be granted until land compensation is complete. Another major impediment is that loan amounts are based on property valuation at state frame prices, which fall significantly below the market value. Firm #8 cited an example: it bought land for 150,000—200,000 VND/sqm, but the bank would only value it at 50,000/sqm. The firms that did borrow from banks financed small portions of their projects. For example, firm #4 noted that it gets bank loans for small projects that involve building one or two villas inside the city but uses customer deposits for big projects on the periphery. Firm #5 financed 10% of its project budget with a formal bank loan. Furthermore, two of the firms preferred to borrow from foreign banks. Firm #6 borrowed from DC Bank in Hong Kong, and Firm #11 borrowed from banks from its native Taiwan. State-owned banks used to discriminate against private firms, offering less favorable terms than they did to state-owned and equitized real estate companies. Several firms reported that obtaining loans depended on one's relationship with the bank and the type of project.

These capital constraints shape the kinds of projects that are developed. Several firms mentioned that it is important they do projects with short turnaround times. This strategy results in projects that consist of serviced lots rather than built houses. But these lower-priced products also fit with the savings levels of customers, most of whom find formal bank mortgages too expensive. They can pay for urban land by installment, and can build houses to their own liking slowly over time. Or they can easily resell it for large capital gains. Another physical impact of this system of financing is that it supports the development of large projects with homogeneous units. This practice helps developers achieve economies of scale, and it reduces the transaction costs of dealing with many customers.

Permits and Approvals

The next step in the development process is navigating the complicated approvals needed from a labyrinth of bureaus, some of which are shown in table 3.2. The timeliness with which a firm completes this step affects a project's feasibility and profitability.

As discussed earlier, over the course of transition the government's practical authority over land management has devolved to the districts. While formally there is strong central government management over most commercial land development projects, in practice, for most medium sized projects of 1–5 hectares, the Prime Minister's Office can be expected to approve what the district approves. Although still difficult, the permitting procedures have in fact improved considerably from the early days of transition, when firms could wait years for approval. There were significant differences in processing permits based on who is applying. Private developers were viewed with suspicion, and found that gaining approval was uncertain in the early years of transition. Now, however, private developers are becoming more accepted, and the development process more stable. In addition to improvements in policies and procedures, the firms found ways to cope.

The investor groups, as well as a few of the professional developers, used the services of consulting companies to expedite the process. One construction and real estate consultant said that competition between consulting companies has been fierce, since there were fewer customers after the Asian currency crisis. Between 1994 and 1996 his company had about

Table 3.2   Permits and approvals involved in urban land development
in Ho Chi Minh City, 2001

1.	Chief Architect's Office approves that proposal conforms to the city's master plan.
2.	Site location survey by Department of Land and Housing.
3.	District's People's Committee contacts the ward.
4.	Ward approves land use right application.
5.	Ward surveys the site.
6.	District's People's Committee requests approval from the Chief Architect's Office and the city's People's Committee to use the site.
7.	Submit feasibility study to Chief Architect's Office and a general project design plan, at scale 1:2,000, with the infrastructure and public amenities shown.
8.	Infrastructure system agreement.
9.	Environmental protection agreement.
10.	Fire protection agreement.
11.	Conceptual design agreement.
12.	Submit feasibility study to the Department of Planning and Investment.
13.	Coordinate a land compensation plan with the district's urban administration bureau and the Department of Finance and Market Prices.
14.	Submit project documents to the Department of Land and Housing for examination.
15.	Project documents forwarded to the national General Department of Land Administration for examination.
16.	Project documents then forwarded to the Prime Minister's Office for approval to give the land use certificate to the firm.
17.	Department of Planning and Investment issues investment license.
18.	Chief Architect's Office and district's People's Committee issues construction permit.
19.	Submit detailed plan at 1:500.
20.	Site landmark.[a]
21.	Pay Land Use Right Fee.
22.	Building Ownership and Land Use Certificate (BOLUC) for each subdivided parcel is issued.

[a]This term refers to what is known as an approval day, when the investors and representatives from the Department of Land and Housing, the ward, the district, and the Chief Architect's Office go to the site with the planned land parcel map before it is built. As a public act, they place boundary markers and pay fees. After the project has been developed, each parcel receives its own certificate, which the developers can sell in the market.

200 customers a year, many of them foreign. Now it had about 30–40 Vietnamese customers a year. About 30% of its clients are now private companies, and most of the projects are in the new districts in the urban periphery. The vice-director stated that they have an advantage because they know the master plan. Nevertheless, he complained about the red tape involved in processing permits.

With consulting firms, project approval for a site could take from six months to one year, depending on the clarity of the original title documents. Construction permits could take two months, an improvement over the six-month to one-year period that it took before 1999. When firms use these consulting companies, which charge between 1% and 2% of the project budget for their services, they can hand over to them the handwritten contracts and receipts of land purchase. Firms #1, #3, and #4 used consulting companies. Firm #2 hired one for a project that had more complicated infrastructure development issues with neighboring parcels but otherwise pursued the approval process themselves.

Other firms did not outsource the processing of permits and approvals but set up a department within their organization to do this work. For Firm #5's Planning and Investment Department, it took one month to receive project approval and approximately one to three years to receive the land use certificate. For Firm #8 it took between six months and one year to receive project approval, improving over the two to three years it used to take before 1999. Firm #9 needed approximately one year to get the Prime Minister's approval for its very large projects of 26–80 hectares.

More influential than employing a consulting company were a firm's political connections and ability to build interpersonal connections with those involved. For example, two small firms, Firms #2 and #12, did not use consulting companies to process the paperwork. Rather, the leaders did the legwork themselves. Firm #2 had originally designated a member who is a businessman to process the approvals. But he could not effectively obtain the approvals, so another leader who already had connections and strong interpersonal skills took over the task. His view was that the right "spirit" of how to treat people and conveying a helpful attitude establishes the trust to ease approvals more effectively than bribes or hometown connections.

On the other hand, the Vietnamese-American leader of Firm #12—who apparently did not have this spirit of Vietnamese capitalism and did not engage any of the available institutional arrangements—took five years to get project approval, one year to get a construction permit, and two years to get the land use certificates, by far the longest of all the firms I studied. For Firm #12, the paperwork was an extraordinarily difficult part of the development process. This firm did not want to hire a consulting company because of the fees. Instead, the founder hired staff to work at getting approvals from the Chief Architect's Office. They found that although their own architects had designed their project, they had to hire a local architect in order to get the project approved. The firm's director complained that his site was surveyed eight times and that it cost him $1,000 USD each time. He said that he did not pay any bribes or spend time building personal relationships with officials.

One institutional arrangement that is exceptional to HCMC is the establishment of the Management Authority for Southern Area Development of Ho Chi Minh City (MASD). The foreign joint-venture Firm #11, after years of lobbying the central and city governments, finally secured support for this special arrangement in processing permits and approvals. In 1998 the Prime Minister established MASD, a special government office housed within HCMC's Department of Planning and Investment, to handle project approval and permits in the southern portion of the city, where Firm #11 has exclusive rights. Its authority is directly under the city's People's Committee and is higher than any district's. MASD is a one-stop service place that coordinates the approvals a developer would normally need to get from the Department of Planning and Investment, Chief Architect's Office, and the Department of Construction. MASD is staffed with around 50 people and is organized into six departments: construction, investment, financing, land, environment and infrastructure, and administration. Firms that would like to develop projects in this area can secure their project approval in one month and their construction permit in another month.

Even with HCMC's expedited procedures and variety of institutional arrangements, waiting to receive formal approval before starting construction was still too risky. Within a year, the land price in their project site could increase significantly. I found in a survey of land prices I conducted that the average price of land increased over 24% between 2000 and 2001, with a very wide standard deviation on the urban periphery (Kim 2004). As a consequence, firms usually started buying land before the project was formally approved by the Prime Minister. According to Firm #8, starting prematurely is encouraged by the district and ward authorities because once a project has passed their approval, the Prime Minister's approval is often a formality, and through their informal communications they can gauge the progress of the final approval. And the law actually allowed that "If it is necessary to level the ground early in order to carry out the project, the council (of Compensation for Damage in Ground Clearance) may be set up before the decision to recover the land (by the state)."[4] Firm #9 said, "In business, time is valuable; you can't wait around for things to go step by step. It affects social efficiency and the supply of housing."

On average, the firms took about two to three years to complete their residential projects. The outlier exception is Firm #12, which did not engage institutional arrangements or social networks. Also, as we saw earlier, some of the firms' projects stalled indefinitely after land compensation negotiations reached an impasse, as was seen in the case of Firm #2's project in Thu Duc District.

Succeeding as an Entrepreneur in Ho Chi Minh City

The previous section described the challenges that firms faced in HCMC and the variety of ways that my case firms devised to overcome them. We saw that political connections and social networks are an integral part because they connected firms to intermediaries and other institutional arrangements such as the many landbrokers and consulting companies whose services were for sale in HCMC. Firms were able to engage the help of those with information and influence to find land, form a larger pool of financing, and expedite development.

But some firms were more successful than others at surviving in HCMC's economic environment. While I argued in chapter 2 that people with varying levels of political and cultural capital became the first generation of real estate developers in HCMC, another question in the transition to capitalism concerns whether political elites are the ones who benefit disproportionately. Do they manipulate the institutional transition to effectively ensure their elite position in the new economy?

To answer this question, I investigated what distinguished the more successful firms from the less successful ones. While the previous section displayed the breadth of strategies and institutional mechanisms that arose during the transition, it is useful to connect these actions with outcomes. My approach is to first determine whether the firms with greater political privilege had better outcomes, then to compare the outcomes of firms that started business with similar political privilege and social positions to find what might be sources of variation. I compare the two equitized companies and then compare three foreign joint-ventures. Finally, I will summarize what was common among the five most productive firms and the two companies that failed, ending their investments in urban land development in HCMC.

In table 3.3, we see a good distribution in the case firms' productivity levels. While profitability would have been a more ideal measure of firm success, I could not insure the quality of financial information and the parity of metrics between the firms. But given the high demand conditions, the supply shortage, the openness of market entry and exit, the similarity in developed units, and the fact that all of their products sold quickly, we can assume that firms were profitable and that productivity provided

Table 3.3   Case firms organized by number of units produced

Low productivity firms Total units <100	Medium productivity firms Total units 100–600	High productivity firms Total units >600
Firms #1, #4, #12, N1, N2	Firms #2, #6, #7, #10	Firms #3, #5, #8, #9, #11

Table 3.4   Case firms organized by size of firm

Small firms <10 employees	Medium firms 10–20 employees	Large firms >20 employees
Firms #1, #2, #3, #8, #12	Firms #4, #5, #6, #7	Firms #9, #10, #11

a good proxy for measuring the ability of firms to operate in HCMC's challenging economic environment. As we saw in the previous section, their productivity depended on their ability to find developable land, quickly clear the land of occupants, gather development financing, and expedite permits and approvals.

We can observe in table 3.4 that the relative size of the firms did not correlate with their productivity levels. There was some correlation between the political connections the firms had, as identified by the social position of the firm's leaders. The cases that are most interesting are Firms #3, #5, and #8, which were of modest size and yet were able to produce many units. Firms #3 and #5 were private companies with exceptional political connections, which certainly helped them attain development control of sites more easily and expedited permitting and approvals. Political connections were necessary, but insufficient to explain the variation in production levels. Firm #10 had some of the strongest political connections of all of the case firms, but it was not one of the star performers. When we examine the operations of the firms more closely, we find that Firms #3 and #5 could develop such large projects because they could move beyond their immediate social networks. For example, Firm #3 was able to organize and collect down payments from nearly 500 people, even though it was an informal, investor group firm. Similarly, Firm #5 was able to attract a regular inflow of new customers to buy into their projects early.

This distinction also comes up when we compare the two equitized firms, #9 and #10, which enjoyed by far the strongest political connections because they had been a part of state-owned enterprises. They were similar in that both equitized in 1999 and they had a similar proportion of shareholders who were government employees and private citizens. One of the biggest differences I noticed between the two equitized firms was the disparity in office cultures.

When I visited Firm #10, it was like stepping into some of the government offices I had visited. There were large rooms filled with desks and people sitting around not doing much of anything. Their chief of marketing explained to me that they equitized from being a state-owned construction company under the city's Department of Land and Housing, giving them special advantages in access to land and approvals. She also said, however, that the main motivations for the firm to equitize were to enjoy tax breaks, to provide the managers with undervalued shares at low cost, to have access to more private capital, and to improve the efficiency of company operations. But she mentioned the latter was "a challenge because it was a totally new pattern. Some people's capacity is limited." They ended up not decreasing the number of employees, who numbered 460. Their approach to business was rather academic. For example, they attempted to assess market demand by conducting a contingent valuation survey once a year instead of gathering data about the thousands of actual market transactions that were happening around them.

In contrast, Firm #9's office was constantly busy, with potential customers coming in to look at maps of new development projects, on which the remaining parcels were marked with a highlighter. The offices were rather spartan and displayed only the necessary pieces of information for customers, which worked to convey a serious bottom line. When I conducted interviews with the vice-director of the firm who actively managed the projects, he was constantly giving brief replies to assistants who were seeking his direction by phone and in person. This former equitized company had shed the usual formal, hierarchical modes of intraoffice communication through written and approved letters.

While Firm #9 had equitized from RESCO, giving it many advantages, it did not rest on its special access to land and expedited project approval. It pursued projects in districts where it had no previous relations. The firm sent letters to ward chairmen and the ward and district officers in charge of land administration to ask for appointments. Although Firm #9 had privileges, its leaders kept aggressively trying to improve its operations, and eventually it became the largest producer of residential land at that time. I attributed many of these differences to the vice-director. His approach was to continually learn. He said that while he had taken a course on business, his real training came from experience and from travel. For example, he recounted that he had traveled to the United States and visited real estate companies, pretending to be a potential Japanese customer in order to see how they tried to market real estate to him. The firm advertised throughout the city on billboards, at property centers, and in newspapers, and its sales force actively pursued potential customers.

A comparison of the difference in outcomes between the foreign joint-ventures also points to the importance of entrepreneurs' and their organizations' ability to learn and change. When the Asian currency crisis hit the region, the large foreign conglomerates, Firms #11 and N2, both scrambled to cope with their sunk costs in Vietnamese land. They had both been early entrants into the Vietnamese economy, and after years of making infrastructure investments at a loss to gain trust and support of authorities, these two firms had negotiated with the city and national governments exclusive and unprecedented development rights for land in HCMC. Both planned to develop upscale commercial projects for the foreign investors who were flowing in, and also to develop their own export-oriented projects. But when the currency crisis hit the region, their pool of capital dried up.

Both wanted to pull out of their investment commitments, like the many other foreign investors who were exiting Vietnam during this time. However, because of the land transfer restrictions, they could not liquidate their investment, which is one of the risks for early entrants into transition economies.

Ultimately, Firm #11 was able to move forward and actually flourish in its operations while N2 stayed at a standstill. The difference was that Firm #11 altered its investment strategy to go down-market and concentrate on using its assets to sell developed property to the local housing market, and to build smaller projects incrementally. This strategy represented a complete change in view and business plan from the commercial and export industries on which it had been focusing. But after the firm developed one successful apartment building, it then experimented with new product types that would meet the demand and pocketbooks of the emerging Vietnamese bourgeoisie. The firm invested in hiring a full-time staff person to constantly gauge market demand throughout the city, it surveyed visitors to their sales offices to see what product would have better met their needs, and it conducted aggressive advertising campaigns, such as arranging for cars with loudspeakers to drive around town touting the firm and its products. In subsequent visits to this firm and the Taiwanese investors behind it, I found that they were no longer pioneering in the farm area outside of HCMC. The firm's development site had exploded, with thousands of units being developed alongside landscaped thoroughfares; their sales office was in a frenzy on weekends with Vietnamese eager to buy into these suburban developments. It also catered to the expatriates who began to return to Vietnam once foreign investment started growing. The investors now sat comfortably in their position as the premier real estate tycoons of not only HCMC, but Vietnam.

Meanwhile, Firm N2 has also managed to gain exclusive land rights in HCMC, but it persisted during the Asian currency crisis with the strategy of building one large, commercial project, just as it had done in other emerging economies. The firm halted construction on the project midway, not tapping into the domestic market. I noticed that firms with foreign experience could sometimes be at a disadvantage working in HCMC if they tended to stay with imported business models and ways of doing business. This situation was also a problem for the much smaller Firm #12, headed by a Vietnamese-American. Although he had formed some connections to the political elite, he attempted to develop the project without engaging any of the available institutional arrangements or intermediaries, and as a result it took eight years to process all the paperwork. He conducted business in Vietnam just as he had in Texas.

One of Firm #4's leaders, who had originally helped found Firm N1 but left when its financial mismanagement became apparent, summarized three lessons he had learned about what was crucial for a firm to be successful in Vietnam's real estate industry: 1) the firm's members must be hardworking; 2) the firm must build a good reputation—customer trust will make it easier to mobilize development financing, but it can also lead to bankruptcy unless it is well invested and not scattered for other purposes; 3) people on the board and in the sales department must understand real estate finance and continually learn from their experience and update their knowledge of market conditions.

This insider's views bear out in the comparison of this study's case firms. While social networks and political connections were important for a firm to operate and develop projects, the most productive firms in table 3.1 moved beyond their immediate networks and made considerable investments in sales and marketing to the general public. This was key to maintaining the steady flow of development capital for their projects. Another characteristic the successful firms showed was their predisposition to learn and make changes in their investment strategies, product types, and business model. The unproductive firms, both domestic and foreign, despite some having advantages in initial capitalization and political connections, shared an inability to adjust to changes in market conditions and to build appropriate institutional arrangements.

Notes

1. For a discussion of methods, see chapter 1 and the appendix.

2. Some firms also combined nonmarket considerations in choosing project sites. For example, Firm #11 decided to locate in the part of HCMC where Taiwanese predecessors had planned to invest before the Vietnam War, despite the area being geologically challenged and completely lacking in infrastructure. Nevertheless, Firm #11 also conducted the most systematic market research of all of the firms, in order to develop specific projects within this district of the city.

3. By cross-subsidizing, this firm was able to develop an affordable housing project that targeted local teachers, who were offered mortgages from the Asia Commercial Bank with favorable terms.

4. Quoted from Article 34 of Decree No. 22/1998/ND-CP, April 24, 1998 with clarifications entered in parentheses.

Part II

Institutional Change

4

The Social Construction of Entrepreneurs

The previous chapter focused on individual entrepreneurs and firms and how each managed to develop urban land in Ho Chi Minh City. It introduced the point that cognitive processes were at play in order for them to become entrepreneurs. They had to learn new ways of thinking and behaving, especially in order to succeed. But it also made the point that this learning was not an individual act but was shaped by their society, since being a private real estate developer in HCMC required the cooperation of many other actors and intermediaries.

In our discussion of the individual entrepreneurs' activities, we have not yet questioned why there were four major development steps to overcome in the first place. By focusing on individual agents, we also could not get a sense of what the entrepreneurs were doing as a group to change the economy and society. While I emphasized in the previous chapter that a wide variety of characters became entrepreneurs and that they were developing land around the city through a variety of means, they were all entrepreneurs and fundamentally changing the shape of the city, the way housing was created, and economic relationships in society. Now I will shift the viewpoint away from individual entrepreneurs and examine the firms as a group in order to explore the process of institutional change.

This chapter shows how the entrepreneurs could not have become entrepreneurs unless the rest of society had changed with them. That is, for people to know whom to go to for housing, what to expect from them, and how to interact with them, all parties had to possess a shared understanding of the new paradigm. We find that the terms of the new roles and relationships involved a society-wide negotiation process that represented a change in social cognition; this change was key to HCMC's transition.

The process of changing social cognition requires us to examine the power dynamics and struggles taking place in the city. Power has sometimes been defined as coercion and intended influence that can constrain and enable human action (Wrong 1995)—a type of institution such as the police power of the state. This definition suggests a duality between the powerful and the weak. However, in contrast to the developmental states of the East Asian miracle economies of an earlier generation, Vietnam has a strong state but one that did not direct private firms or the national economy in the same way. This chapter recounts the multifaceted expressions of power, including the protest and participation of the less powerful, in reconstructing the market.

The new market paradigm that was socially negotiated was significantly different from the conventional paradigm of how real estate investments and markets are supposed to happen. That is, a Vietnamese variety of capitalism emerged through the social construction process. These findings suggest that solving the puzzle of transition requires us to reconsider the role of cognition in institutional change. A framework is proposed at the end of this chapter and is employed in the next chapter to explain the variation we observe in other transition cases.

Fiscal Socialism: Power and the Vietnamese Variety of Capitalism

My case firms were an eclectic group in terms of size and productivity, ownership structure, domestic and foreign participation, political power, and social position. I later realized, however, that they all shared a common understanding of the new social reality and the way private land development happens in HCMC. Furthermore, this new order was not outlined in any government economic development plan, nor did it conform to any urban economics textbook model of how urban land markets function. Still, after my fieldwork, in the course of which I interviewed and observed many people inside and outside the firms involved in the newly emerged private real estate market, I was able to diagram the system. When I revisited my case firms in 2004, I showed the diagram to their leaders as well as other key informants to test my interpretation of the roles and the terms of the new economic relationships. They all confirmed that the diagram was accurate, and one developer further explained that this knowledge is what distinguished firms like his from what he called "those ridiculous people" who think they are real estate developers because they construct something on land. The motley group of entrepreneurs I studied possessed this new and shared cognitive paradigm.

Figure 4.1 represents how the real estate market functions in HCMC and the constellation of interests that supports the

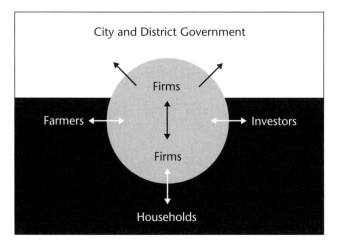

Figure 4.1 The new Vietnamese housing market paradigm: Fiscal Socialism.

system. I call this constellation of interests fiscal socialism. In the private housing market, the state looms large. The white area represents the public realm, where the HCMC government and its district governments own and control most of the developable land in the city. But while they have announced vague project plans for the land in the periphery, they do not have the public finance to implement most of their proposals. Without institutions such as an effective property or income tax system, the state has not yet developed institutions to extract substantial financial capital from the private sector for public works. The black area represents the private sector, which includes households wanting to buy houses or serviced land plots, farmers who are currently occupying land that will be developed, and private investors who are looking to invest the surplus they accumulated during the initial years of transition.[1]

Between this divide is the gray, amorphous sphere of the private land development organizations. These firms do not fit neatly into either the public or private sectors. They may actually have state employees or former state employees who still exercise their influence as part of their organization. But they are not state-owned enterprises, and they exercise autonomy in project identification and operations. The firms broker between the land resources controlled by the government authorities and the financial capital available in the private sector. They develop the urban land parcels serviced with infrastructure services that all parties seek. They do not provide all of the financing for the projects with their equity, but negotiate deals for additional financing from the private sector.

This Vietnamese market has several notable characteristics. Parties are willing to risk engaging in this system despite weak property rights protection. The state leverages land control by giving official permission to develop the land and titles for the subdivided parcels to firms after they have developed the property. Meanwhile, the firms' customers buy into the project early in the development process, providing construction financing to the firms before they have seen the property, even though courts are not widely accessible to enforce sales contracts.

The use of land as currency is another characteristic of this land development system. While investors contribute equity to the project, some of it comes in the form of undeveloped land that they have secured which assists the difficult process of land consolidation at the project site. While some investors receive their returns in the form of financial payments, some prefer to receive developed parcels, as these will continue to appreciate in value. In addition, as we will see later in this chapter, farmers are increasingly given developed parcels as compensation for relocating.

Another characteristic of HCMC's real estate market is that we find more coordination than competition between the firms. For example, firms will divide up portions of a larger project to develop, or locate projects adjacent to one another, in order to save on the development cost of infrastructure. This strategy is represented in figure 4.1 by the arrows within the gray sphere of the private firms. In the traditional view, a lack of competition would indicate an inefficient market. From the firms' accounts, however, while entering the market does involve transaction and information costs, market entry is open. Cooperation between firms is sustained by the huge and growing housing demand and the availability of developable land, allowing more firms to enter without decreasing the business of others. This phenomenon is not so unusual, given that other case studies of successful Asian economies have indicated high levels of interfirm networking and close business-government relations (Amsden 1989; Wade 2004).

Understanding the unusual characteristics of HCMC's housing market requires recognizing how power dynamics influence institutional change. In the fiscal socialism system, not surprisingly, the state plays a large role. As outlined in chapter 2, the state has considerable coercive power in Vietnam, and it has structured a specific economic space for private land development through land ownership and urban planning controls. The state shaped where developers could do projects as well as project scale. But its authority also removed many risks for the firms once they received its support, including tying down development control over land, assisting them through the state's own labyrinthine approval and permitting process, and negotiating land compensation deals. In effect, the state promoted private land development by retaining significant control over land.

In fact, the state's power is so strong, and political connections are so important in urban land development, that it might at first blush seem that its interests determine everything. We know from the accounts of developmental states in Japan, South Korea, and Singapore that the state seemed to pick firms to work the capitalist economy (Amsden and Singh 1994; Yu 1997; Wade 2004; Stiglitz 1996). However, a major difference from the earlier generation of miracle economies is that the Vietnamese central government decentralized much of its authority over development approval and planning to the HCMC government and the city's district governments. This decentralization has enabled considerable discretion and variability in the design and accessibility of land development plans and the terms of project approvals.[2] As area studies scholars argue, even though Vietnam's authoritarian government is capable of suppressing political opposition and monitoring the population, it has had limited ability to actually promote development and transform the economy. Even while the state might severely constrain the location of development, it can no longer command investment and production to happen. Instead, these scholars posit that a bottom-up, social phenomenon motivated new activity (Fforde and de Vylder 1996; Fforde and Luong 1996; Gainsborough 2002b, 2005). This phenomenon does not mean that state power is absent, however, but that rather than focusing on the central government, in Vietnam one needs to examine the coordination of interests operating at all levels of government and society (Gainsborough 2002a).

What interests would be served by various state bureaus becoming more amenable to private real estate companies after initially discriminating against them? In particular, why would the district governments so actively help firms to succeed? Conversely, why would any private citizen attempt this new economic activity? Why would they work in such a constrained environment that makes it risky to realize profit? The answers to these questions lie in the complex strategic alignment of interests in fiscal socialism.

> Try as it might, the housing sector in burgeoning Ho Chi Minh City simply cannot keep up with demand. Over the last two decades, the population in the city increased 50 per cent while construction of residential areas rose only 25 per cent.... While speed of construction fails to keep pace with population growth, the city's infrastructure lags both. Some newly-built living quarters have been put into use without water supplies or drainage systems and rely on underground water. Electricity and water supply per capita is also on the decrease. Not only is Ho Chi Minh City the nation's most densely-populated city but it also contains the largest number of slum dwellings—67,000 in total, 24,000 of which are located on or near seriously polluted water canals. (Hong 2000)

With transition, intergovernmental relations fundamentally changed when economic planning was decentralized to local governments. This decentralization meant that with HCMC's rapid and unstoppable urbanization, local government faced a dilemma. It had almost no independent revenue raising authority or expenditure allocation autonomy, since tax rates and spending are determined by the national assembly. Yet it is the local government that must manage the new population growth and provide public services. More specifically, there is a housing shortage and increasing need for infrastructure development.

In the early years of Vietnam's transition, the state focused on attracting foreign investment. Vietnam's limited pool of domestic capital sought joint investment projects with foreign firms in which the Vietnamese partner's main contribution would be land use rights. With the Asian currency crisis in 1997, however, foreign investment dropped precipitously. This drop had a large impact on real estate development in HCMC. Much of the previous investment in real estate had focused on high-end commercial space and industrial zones. By the late 1990s, downtown HCMC was littered with stalled commercial real estate projects. As I mentioned in the previous chapter, two of my foreign joint-venture case firms also tried to follow the mass exodus of foreign investors from Vietnam, but they could not work themselves out of the heavy investments they had made in land rights. In an ironic counterpoint to the aim of economic liberalization reforms, foreign divestment contributed to the domestic housing market's rapid growth in HCMC. The silver lining in the currency crisis for Vietnam's urban areas was that as foreign partners left town, domestic investors were more willing to shift their capital into the huge domestic demand for housing and urban development.[3]

In fiscal socialism, a play on "fiscal federalism," the cities, and in particular district governments, leverage land control to raise public finance and provide public services. Firm #5's internal memo describes the situation:

> Government as infrastructure buyer is a hard-to-please customer. [The] [s]olution is that land transfer has been done in the form of a begging-granting mechanism which requires experience in dealing and handling the situation. The procedure is complicated as [approval is needed from] many levels of authority[;] it requires experience and good business relationships, resulting in higher costs and more time-consuming. [sic]

The leader of Firm #9 explained, "Real estate is not just business; it's politics. It is effective to use small companies because they have enormous capital but can't get legal permission to use land for big projects." Firms, unlike individuals, can implement projects with economies of scale sufficiently large to develop the public infrastructure and utilities. City district governments were much more amenable to private developers than the central government, and they especially sought the participation of these firms. Some firms reported that district officials approached them with specific land parcels for purchase and development. Others recounted instances when the district government helped them in other ways, such as convincing the Chief Architect's Office to alter the zoning of housing types from villas to rowhouses, which would be more profitable.

Also reflected in the developers' statements is that while working with the various government bureaus is not easy, the interaction is characterized as a negotiation rather than a command. While the firms complained about the government's requests to build public amenities, infrastructure improvements located near their projects would also increase their property values. The statements also indicate that firms needed to do much more than financial analysis. They needed to learn how to operate in this environment and work with specific agents. This knowledge did not come naturally, but through experience and relationships.

The diagram of fiscal socialism, figure 4.1, essentially outlines how the interests aligned among the state, firms, and consumers. The firms sit at the intersection of the local government's fiscal constraints and society's demand for more urban housing. The city has announced vague project plans for most of the developable land in the periphery, but clearly it will not be able to finance or implement most of it. Meanwhile, a large and ever-growing number of households who seek better housing on this land need to spread out their payments. As in the rest of the world, the cost of housing is so large relative to the average household's income that financing is required. But in Vietnam, only a small portion of households can access mortgage financing because the terms are not affordable to most of the population.[4] As explained in the previous chapter, the predominant method of financing project construction has been to collect prepayments from household customers starting with a 30% downpayment. In the face of the huge housing demand and the scarcity of parcels with land use titles in HCMC, households are willing to pay installments before construction begins. Thus private firms, unlike the state, are able to access household savings derived from rising incomes.

These prepayments by customers are an important source of development capital for these firms. The lending practices of state-owned banks have discriminated against private firms. And while newly emerged private banks are interested in offering mortgages to end-user households, they are not yet willing to offer substantial project financing, and their interest rates are still too high to be attractive to most companies. During my interviews with Asia Commercial Bank's president, vice president, and manager, they said that they had no intention of starting construction lending at the time because of the high risks involved. The potential client firms typically have little equity. Furthermore, under guidelines from the State Bank of Vietnam, their collateral would be undervalued based on the state frame prices, which might be only 50–60% of market value. Bank representatives also mentioned that they do not want to repeat neighboring Thailand's 1997 fiscal crisis.

The local government is supportive of this arrangement because through the state's control of land, officials can require that developers build the infrastructure it has planned in exchange for approval of their project and the administration of land titles, for which the developer can charge a premium to customers because of their scarcity (Kim 2004). Development exactions include roads, pavement, concrete sewer and drainage pipes, water supply, electricity, landscaping, and facilities such as schools. Infrastructure development can account for 50–60% of the budget for projects producing serviced lots. Often, the firms hire the state-owned construction companies to develop the infrastructure to connect to existing grids and conform to design standards.

Fiscal socialism means that the firms and consumers bear all of the development risk. The firms may start construction and begin selling parcels, only to find that the project will not be approved or that land compensation negotiations have stalled. Consumers may pay for houses that are delayed in construction, rising in price, or never built. Because the official transfer and titling of the properties occurs at the end of construction, which is financed along the way by customers and the firms' equity, the sunk costs provide some incentives for the developer and the customer to stay with the project as problems arise. The unabated growth of property values also acts as a deterrent in leaving the project. However, in order to work, this system requires detailed coordination between local government and the firms and effective intergovernmental communication. If all goes smoothly, fiscal socialism produces public infrastructure, the local government bolsters its legitimacy, the firms make a profit, and citizens can purchase houses that are better than what they had in the centrally planned economy.

Property rights are titled in the final stage of the development process rather than as a precondition for investment. In light of this, one can see that conventional reform programs, which would distance the public and private sector and distribute clear title throughout the city, would not allow urban land to be developed through this system. Unless firms and households can build up their assets and formal bank financing becomes more accessible, fiscal socialism provides a way to finance urban development. This system may not represent the ideal institutional framework, but it is the one that emerged.

Resistance and the Shaping of Social Cognition

The developers' roles and actions, then, were shaped by the strategic alignment of interests within society: local government legitimacy and public finances, developer profits, increased housing supply for consumers, and investment opportunities for private capital. Even though Vietnam had a strong, one-party state, the government could not dictate, and indeed fiscal socialism arose because the state could no longer finance production. Power was not confined to a person or organization; rather, we find that the structural forces of power flows through the alignment of a wider group of interests (Foucault 1976).

But certainly not everyone's interests were well served by fiscal socialism. This study would be remiss if it did not include the social debate and violent land protests that were an intimate part of Vietnam's transition to a private housing market. The fiscal socialism system hinges on land control, made plainly apparent in the social discord over land conversions, especially by the rural poor. More recent scholarly treatments of power emphasize that understanding institutionalized power requires examination of the resistance against it in order to identify its limits and inconsistencies. Furthermore, resistance is observable not only in physical acts and protests but also in people's narratives about resistance, which become embedded in society's stream of sociocultural knowledge (Silbey and Ewick 2003). This implies, then, that during times of institutional change such as economic transition, the less powerful can have an important part in reshaping social cognition—the changing roles and relationships in the economy. Within the constraints of Vietnam's political economy, the farmers' repertoire of resistance included public complaints and editorials, increasing the compensation price, and foot-dragging and holding out in negotiations. These acts of resistance helped to construct new narratives in society that fueled an eventual change in how business was conducted.[5] Most significantly, they gained an increased ability to negotiate the terms of land transfer with the developers and the government and to temporarily slow the rate of urban land development in the city.

The lack of attention paid to the role of the less powerful members of society is a major omission in the transition economics literature. The initial studies of transition tended to focus on the state, its reforms, ideologies, politicians, and so forth, when the transition involved privatization of the economy. In contrast, some comparative capitalism studies began to examine entrepreneurs and firms in the newly emerged private sector. Scholars such as Burawoy (2001), however, deride "trendy" scholars who privilege elites, such as entrepreneurs and politicians, by making them the study of transition. He argues that focusing on elites will not account for the observed varieties of capitalism because their variation may lie in the way elites have been effectively constrained by non-elites through the "voice" of protestors and their "exit" into the informal economy.[6] He also criticizes 'neoclassical sociologists,' who have missed the critical issues of power and domination by marveling at capitalism's emergence in the most unlikely of places. Leading sociologists have countered that the old Marxist paradigm of class struggle does not explain well the phenomenon of transition since a working class movement has not formed (Eyal, Szelenyi, and Townsley 2001; Stark and Bruszt 2001). In the case of the Asian transitions, however, there has been significant conflict between social groups, in particular the rural population, urban elites, and local governments. In the case of Vietnam, I agree with Burawoy that we cannot have a good understanding of transition without accounting for the protests and dissent that have emerged despite the state's political repression, since these forces have actually impacted the process of institutional change.

For most of the transition, the firms had the upper hand in negotiations with farmers. If the project fit the master plan and had been approved, the local government bodies generally helped the developer in the compensation negotiations with the current owner. They formed a negotiation group called Council of Compensation for Damage in Ground Clearance (Hoi Dong Den Bu), was headed by representatives from the district, and included representatives from the ward, the firm, the Fatherland Front, and the Department of Finance and Market Prices, along with two representatives from the farmers' association. The assertion of low compensation levels by the firm and districts was assisted by official state requirements. The Department of Finance and Market Prices publishes formulas for compensation to be paid to those relocated. Its calculations are based on the location of the site, the quality of property being dismantled, and the proof and length of tenancy. The formula prices were invariably much lower than the market prices, which were growing wildly in the speculative market. These were so low that in fact the developers usually paid higher rates than these published prices, which bolstered their claim that the rates they offered were reasonable.

Farmers were sometimes railroaded into selling at low prices, and there have been several public scandals centering around the way local government officials have managed these land transfers. One of the more notorious cases that occurred during my fieldwork in HCMC concerned a French joint-venture project to build the large Western-style An Lac supermarket in Binh Chanh, a district in the urban periphery. Originally the district gave project approval for 100,000 square meters of land; this space later increased by another 50,000 square meters to accommodate a larger parking lot. Households protested that they were forced to accept low compensation rates, and some eventually became homeless (Quynh 2000b). I saw demonstrators camped out on the sidewalk in front of the city government hall in downtown HCMC. Because passers-by were not allowed to speak to them, they had made large banners with long explanations of their grievances. However, what was surprising was that they were allowed to stay on the major boulevard in HCMC for weeks, until U.S. President Bill Clinton came for his historic visit.

This tolerance for an organized gathering of political dissent was startling in politically repressive Vietnam. In fact, in the late 1990s, public protests about land conversion issues started occurring in various parts of the country. The state-run media was not allowed to cover any violent protests. For example, from May to September of 1997 there was a media blackout on the protests in Thai Binh province near Hanoi, where farmers had protested against local government corruption, punitive taxes, land disputes, compulsory labor contributions, and unfair rice prices. Similarly, in November 1997, foreign journalists were banned from covering violent protests in Dong Nai province, near HCMC, that occurred in response to the local authorities, expropriation of the Catholic church's land in Tra Co commune (Human Rights Watch 1997). Yet in the midst of the local media blackout, international newspapers covering the incidents were widely available in Vietnamese hotels and from street newspaper sellers.

Starting in 1997, however, the major newspapers in HCMC, such as Tuoi Tre (Youth News), Lao Dong (Trade Union), and Thanh Nien (Youth Union), began to publish articles about land disputes that included criticism of local leaders. These stories, which appeared as regularly as weekly or several times a month, criticized district and ward government officials and even the city government. One foreign journalist who worked for six years on the staff of Vietnam News, an English-language newspaper in Vietnam, recounts that in the early days of transition there were no formal regulations in place about censoring news coverage. Rather, it was more a matter of cultural self-censorship.[7] Eventually a major change evolved in public discourse where citizens could publish criticism of local government.[8] And this dissent sometimes produced significant effects. In the case of the An Lac supermarket controversy, the district's People's Committee leaders were reshuffled and a leader demoted.

This opening in public discourse represented just a small part of the power struggle occurring in Vietnam on the cognitive level—different members of society were challenging the received understanding of how major changes would happen in Vietnam's transition. The state defended fiscal socialism by constructing a public interest argument that emphasized economic growth and the relief of urban housing shortages as the top priority. This was balanced by official documents that reemphasized that adequate compensation should be paid to those who were being forced to relocate. Meanwhile, there were a number of oppositional discourses concerning developers, farmers, and the legitimacy of the government that reshaped some of the social facts of fiscal socialism and ultimately the activities of the bureaus and the developers.

Throughout my fieldwork, I often heard sentiments that conveyed a lingering sense of the illegitimacy of profiting through private land development. One former deputy director of a state-owned real estate development company advised me that private developers were not worth researching because they used immoral means to profit. It seemed a bit ironic to me since she had invited me to conduct the interview in her luxurious villa, which was located in one of the projects developed by her state-owned enterprise. But scandals like the Minh

Phung/Epco downfall, in which the leaders of the firm had just been imprisoned, loomed large in the news at the time and furthered the notion that private companies were irresponsible to the public (Gainsborough 2003). Many of my case firms tried to portray themselves as somehow different from greedy, purely capitalist developers and seemed to be attempting to downplay the success of their activities. Firm #3 referred to their work as a "non-business" project even though they were producing over a thousand units that their members could resell. The director of the large equitized Firm #9 saw himself as a sort of affordable housing developer when he pointed out that one or two of his projects reaped no profit and that he was contributing to society, since he had come from humble circumstances himself. In fact, the largest, most successful firms, Firms #9 and #11, also produced lower-income housing projects and public community amenities even though no regulations required them to do so. In contrast, the foreign joint-venture firms did not try to tone down their success or assume egalitarian motives. For example, the American joint-venture emphasized that his firm's projects were for an elite clientele and disdained the thought of building projects for middle- to lower-income Vietnamese. The Taiwanese joint-venture firm matter-of-factly pointed out its dominant position in securing land rights for a large section of the periphery and the innovative ways it was developing projects.

Content analysis of articles from the newspaper Tuoi Tre from 1999 to 2006, however, showed few articles about private investors or land developers, with the exception of the Minh Phung/Epco scandal. Instead, factual news briefs would occasionally announce what a firm was building and the amount of investment. Sometimes these briefs had a slightly positive tone, suggesting progress for the city. But the majority of articles about land issues and controversies were editorials critical of local government officials, portraying them as greedy and corrupt figures who took advantage of their position and did not follow the official regulations. For example, one article described itself as a "portrait of a ward chairman—powerful, profit hungry though selling public land" (Trung 2000). It is not clear what happened to allow this change in the tenor of media coverage. The social movement literature suggests that there are times when agents can take advantage of political opportunities by strategically framing their situation, appealing to the central government's stated policies (for clean government, rule of law, and village level democratic reform) as a shield (Li and O'Brien 1996). An event can spark the reframing of a situation with long-dormant contradictions (Zald 1996). Or if we assume that irregularities in the handling of land conversions are common-place throughout the city, media attention to particular cases and officials may also be a function of internal governmental politics, especially since in Vietnam the state owned all of the media outlets. On the whole, the new permissiveness about crit-icizing local government was a convenient way for the central government to retain its legitimacy while decentralizing to local government the responsibility of urban development.

On the other hand, when I interviewed private people involved with the market, I found that some of them also painted the farm-ers as immoral. One real estate lawyer explained that most of her practice's cases involved disputes over land sale contracts. She said that the farmer sellers are typically "greedy and dishonest," and she helps her customers get their money back when they cannot take possession of the land for which they paid. Landbrokers also called some of the farmers' household members greedy for block-ing sales in the hope of obtaining a higher price.[9]

The social discontent over urban land development was so widespread and carried enough legitimacy that a landmark polit-ical event occurred in 2000. The central government dispatched five legal teams around the country to settle some of the most controversial land disputes. Farmers were given an opportunity to have an audience with them and to present their evidence. In the majority of the cases, the central government represen-tatives sided with the farmers (Quynh 2000c). Previously, com-plaints had to be submitted to the ward and then forwarded to the district, but often these lower-level bureaus would hold the documents and keep petitioners waiting. Now, complaints can be submitted to the central government's office in HCMC.

Another major regulatory development that occurred because of the civil unrest over land compensation controversies was a revision in land compensation regulations. As discussed earlier, Decree 22 gave much authority over the land compensation council to the district authorities who had incentives to help the firms and helped pressure farmers to sell cheaply. In 2004, Decree 197 revised these guidelines giving the city more oversight of this process. It also introduced new language directing the district authorities "to settle citizens complaints, denunciations related to compensation, support and resettlement" and "to guarantee impartiality and equity when considering and deciding on the compensation, support, and resettlement" (Article 43 of Decree 197/2004/ND-CP). As a result, private investors now negotiate directly with the farmers and agree on a price without the active support of local government. Officially, if the negotiations come to an impasse over a parcel that is located within the site of an approved project, the city's People's Committee, in consultation with its Department of Finance and Market Price, can ultimately determine the price. But as a result of Decree 197 and the shifting political tide, the city government has become wary of entering into land compensation negotiations between private firms and farmers. Moreover, other regulations require that firms first reach compensation agreements for about 80% of the project site area before they can receive approval for the land subdivision plan, which the firms need in order to sell parcels in advance to customers. The terms of fiscal socialism have shifted such that individual farmers have the ability to hold up projects by refusing to agree to the price. "If the farmer protests and petitions, the government is on the farmer's side. By law, the state could force them to sell, but so far it is impossible to do," says a veteran developer in Firm #6. In addition, Firm #4 recounts that the real estate market's explosive growth started to flag in 2003 when the district governments lost some autonomy because a new deputy mayor of HCMC came into office and enforced laws and regulations more carefully. The firm's leader describes him as "a real Communist. He has no friends, no relationships, no corruption, no knowledge about business."

The public discourse and the changing regulatory environment affected the firms' project timing, costs, and scale. As we saw in the previous chapter, the timing of negotiations usually varied simply by size of project. Firms #1, #2, #6, and #8 typically took about one month to complete negotiations for projects that were about one hectare in size. The larger projects of Firms #3, #7, #8, #9, and #12 took about six months to two years, depending on the number of farmers and the difficulty of negotiations. Now, since the projects could stall indefinitely over the compensation negotiations, Firm #6 said that if a farmer refused to sell, the firm would sometimes offer a price above market levels. Alternatively, developers faced with stalled land negotiations may choose to reduce the size of the project, assuming that a significant portion of the project site had already been obtained. Finally, developers will sometimes offer developed land units as a form of compensation to the farmers, so that the project size does not have to be reduced as dramatically. Government officials encourage this form of compensation, which gives the farmer a chance to share in the increased appreciation that comes from the urban development of agricultural land. In the post–Decree 197 era, Firm #9 has increasingly pursued this compensation strategy to clear its very large project sites. A journalist who covers real estate issues noted during an interview that he had witnessed the increasing use of this arrangement, which he viewed as the way out of impasse in the future.

These changes in compensation negotiations show that the land transfer situation shifted in response to the pushback from social conflict. Whereas compensation was originally a one-time payment to move farmers, now farmers are increasingly negotiating for a portion of the developed property, asserting their rights to share in the asset-building that has emerged from the fiscal socialism system. In other words, the less powerful still had a role in shaping social cognition and, therefore, the terms of their role in fiscal socialism. We also see the central government distancing itself from the unsavory part of the transition to a land market, even though it helped create this situation by not providing public finance for local government. The central government now permits the general public to vilify district and ward officials, who are easily demoted. The unpopular, politically difficult act of negotiating compensation was offloaded to the developer, who was still expected to build the infrastructure. By 2003, it was apparent that these changes had disrupted the flow of development capital, as customers would not buy into projects that lacked investment approval. Consequently, the firms' production of housing slowed down considerably.

Notes

1. I write "farmers" as shorthand for the current occupants of land that was previously designated for agricultural use but is now planned for urban use. Residents of the urban periphery might not actually be farming their land; some are employed in the urban economy. And as transition progressed, urban, private investors bought up much of the available land, so that now there are few farmers left.

2. China appears to have similarities with the situation described here (Zhu 2002; Li 1999). Scholars emphasize that one of the elements that characterized China's transition was that the state decentralized economic development strategies down to local government. While these are just two countries, they are currently among the fastest growing economies in the world, and the challenges they are making to both the conventional and developmental state models of economic development deserve close examination.

3. "Richard Whybrow, country manager at property consultants Jones Lang Wootton, said Asia's woes held a silver lining for the city because it had halted many speculative projects. 'There was a lot of speculation in the gaining of licenses for property development and if these had gone ahead there would have been massive problems. If the Asian crisis hadn't hit there would have been a frightening amount of oversupply,' he said" (Vietnam Investment Review 1998).

4. Asia Commercial Bank (ACB) is Vietnam's premier joint-stock bank involved in the real estate industry. ACB began residential lending in HCMC in 1997. With 40% of Vietnam's housing mortgages, ACB has the biggest housing portfolio of any bank in the country. By 2001 it had lent about 400 home mortgages of an average loan amount of 205 million VND (roughly $14,000 USD), with late payments on less than 5% of the loans. ACB was very careful in approving borrowers in order to keep loan default rates low, because social norms do not allow foreclosure. (Firm #11 told me that even with some legislative developments, the government "can't get used to the idea of mortgaging, evicting, and foreclosing.") Instead, ACB loans only to the population groups it considers most reliable, such as teachers. It

has also developed mechanisms for enforcing loan repayment that engage social networks and institutional arrangements. If the payment is late less than three months, it sends letters and a bank officer visits the borrower's home. If the payment is more than three months late, it asks the ward officer, to whom it gives small consumer loans, to go to the borrower's house in order to put pressure on them.

5. Changing construction standards represents another example of how firms and governments adjusted practices in response to public pressure. Firm #9 reported that when it was a state-owned enterprise, the city inspections for drainage construction were mere formalities. But now, because of "public response," the inspections are rigorous. The firm tenders bids for construction, which is overseen by the government, and costs are checked and construction supervised.

6. For example, Davis (2004) argues that the rural middle class was a key factor in ensuring that the state disciplined capitalists to produce economic results in South Korea's and Taiwan's rapid economic development, in contrast to Mexico and Argentina.

7. The same former Vietnam News reporter told me that journalists still do not use Ho Chi Minh's name casually, and he noted that there are still two kinds of articles journalists never write: articles that directly criticize Communist Party policies, and articles that try to preempt future policies.

8. For example, in the article "People say, 'We ask for justice,'" (Quynh 2000d), households accuse the city government of not compensating according to regulations. Another article accuses a ward chairman of asking for kickbacks for land compensation for Hiep Phuc Industrial Zone (Quynh 2000a).

9. Another changing social norm is the growing independence in the way that children relate to their parents. People increasingly want to move away from their extended families, fueling the explosive housing demand. A landbroker reported that the most frequent problem she encounters in land negotiations is dissension within the seller's household. Inheritance traditions divide assets among children according to gender and birth order. Sometimes the children claim rights to the land and differ with their parents on the price at which they want to dispose of the land. If one family member disagrees with a sales price, the parcel cannot be sold, because it requires the signatures of all of the owners. The landbroker said that children have sued, making situations very complicated.

5

Social Cognition

The previous three chapters presented how the entrepreneurs in HCMC became entrepreneurs. And yet, many of these findings do not fit well with current conventional ideas about who becomes entrepreneurs, how to promote entrepreneurialism, and the transition to a capitalist economy. Interests, incentives, and structured political privilege were not enough to explain the diversity of outcomes we observed. People do not obey or even react to every change and incentive in their social and economic environment. They respond to some but not to others, and in unexpected ways. Given countervailing and shifting external incentives, particularly in times of major systemic transition, *how* do people choose which incentives in the environment to respond to and what changes in behavior to make?

The importance of cognitive changes kept appearing throughout the developers' accounts and other field data. Other scholars of capitalism have also recently turned their attention to the importance of cognition in economic system change (Greif 2006; Nee and Swedberg 2007; North 2005). They have recognized that cognitive processes can help us explain the variation in economic outcomes that we have seen and locate factors related to the likelihood, type, and rate of economic change.

One of the important issues unaddressed in this nascent literature is how to conceptualize cognition. As it is a fairly recent intellectual innovation to include cognition in economic studies, and since the field of cognitive science is currently experiencing tremendous growth in research findings, it is not surprising that our understanding of the role of cognition in the economy is underdeveloped. What is notable is that economics and business scholars tend to approach cognitive issues as primarily a neuroscience issue. They assume economic actions are influenced by impulses and cognitive processes that are hard-wired in all human beings. With this assumption, one could study agents and generalize behavioral principles at play in the economy. And this fits well with the field of economics' intellectual underpinnings.

However, my findings argue for the need for a socially constructed conception of cognition. With the same cognitive hardware, humans have displayed astounding variation in how they perceive, act, and change actions in their local economies. A major reason for this diversity emanates from the fact that economic transactions are social. Recognizing the importance of how social influences and power dynamics impact cognitive processes is essential to understanding empirical outcomes in the transition economies. In this chapter, I discuss how a wider reading of the cognition literature can improve our understanding of how social, cognitive processes influence economic behavior and institutional change. A social cognition framework better explains how the first generation of land developers emerged in HCMC.

How People Learn and Change

In chapter 3 we learned that the productive firms invested more heavily in market research and sales and marketing, adapted their business model to changing market conditions, created their own institutional arrangements, and extended social networks. Other firms, however, did not. What accounts for this difference? We saw that it was not exactly a function of whether they had political privilege. Rather, they seemed to process their situation differently; the successful firms learned and changed.

This section introduces concepts from cognitive development literature, which will help us understand how the entrepreneurs learned and started changing their behaviors.

Vicarious Learning

One of the major concepts that illuminates how people start to change their behaviors is that of vicarious learning, which suggests that people start to change their behavior as a result of seeing how other people behave.

Bandura (1986) showed with his famous experiment that in contradiction to prevailing theories about genetic predisposition, aggression in children's behavior could be influenced by examples of other children's behavior they saw on television. He went on to develop the influential theory of *social cognition* which laid out how humans learn behavior through cognitive processes which integrate both social influences and agentic choices. His findings were the stimulus for numerous studies of adults in different contexts such as the psychosocial factors influencing the rate of adopting innovations (Rogers 1983). Meanwhile, behavioral finance has also focused on how social, cognitive factors influence economic choices such as the evidence of herd behavior in the marketplace (Scharfstein and Stein 1990). More detailed psychological studies, however, have indicated that people do not necessarily copy other people's behavior but rather acquire tacit knowledge of innovations vicariously. Agents begin to perceive the underlying framework of a model's behavior and then can generate behavior going beyond what they have seen or heard. These new competencies imply agent creativity (Bandura 1997).[1] In the firms' accounts, we found that many of these companies learned from one another as they created the new market institutions.[2]

If a change in actions involves high uncertainties and information is not as accessible, however, people tend to fall back
on simpler rules and ignore incentives to change (Tversky and
Kahneman 1974, 1979). In chapter 3 we saw that some firms that
enjoyed political advantages or had secured special development rights were not as willing to change their business model.
Adapting to the new market conditions, finding a new market
niche, and developing different product types would involve
investment into the unknown. The literature suggests that a
person resists new actions if the innovation conflicts with one's
self-conception. That is, people do not necessarily follow the
herd but may also operate out of their own principles and ideas.
Or, people may follow the herd by changing their principles and
ideas when they encounter cognitive dissonance (Bandura 1986;
Festinger 1957). For example, we saw how developers and other
participants in private real estate tried to justify the profits they
were making within a Communist political system by present-
ing themselves as affordable housing developers or as pursuing
"non-business" projects.

In any case, the latest institutional economics research has
recognized that since in times of major institutional change even
the most rational of agents can no longer follow his or her usual
decision-making processes, agents must learn new paradigms
(Denzau and North 1994). North makes the case that economists
need to further develop a model of "cognitive institutionalism"
in order to understand the process of economic system change
(North 2005; Mantzavinos 2001). In other words, international
development objectives to reform the economy require new patterns of thinking.

Attention

While it is clear that people are influenced by other people, we
do not observe everyone equally. We pay attention to some people more than others because we admire them, or because they
stand out for some other reason. In HCMC, we saw that the
firms paid a great deal of attention to the investment activity

of powerful local people. Meanwhile, in light of international development strategies to import "best practices" it is notable how little influence foreign firms had on Vietnamese business practices. While Firm #9's vice-director was curious to learn how U.S. firms marketed their products, he did not adopt their practices. In fact, the foreign firm that did succeed paid better attention to local practices and conditions and changed its business model, including financing practices and product types.

The literature emphasizes that we have some agency in who or what we pay attention to and even in how we perceive it. Perceptions are not a pure sensory experience. Rather, we belong to a number of "cognitive communities" that shape our attention. Zerubavel (1997) provides interesting examples of how theories in the physical sciences have changed even though the objects of study have stayed constant, such as whether men and women are different sexes, whether light is a particle or a wave, and so forth. Furthermore, people resist acknowledging perceptions that contradict their preexisting models and tend to notice information that supports them. As an example, Zerubavel points out that for three hundred years Europeans worked to maintain their belief that America was actually Asia, or at least connected to Asia, even though both the physical evidence and the statements of native peoples pointed to the opposite conclusion.

Some behavioral finance economists have indicated that the way issues are framed is important in influencing behaviors (Tversky and Kahneman 1981). But the fact that society shapes what we pay attention to is not well recognized by development or evolutionary economists who still assume a positivistic cognitive process. In their accounts, we construct mental models, and when we encounter facts in the environment that contradict our models, we should adapt them. But there are many possible things that might be noticed that go unnoticed. We have limited cognitive abilities, and society has shaped what we think is and is not noteworthy. Once we acknowledge the social influence on our perceptions and interpretations, we move a long way toward integrating agent cognitive functions with social structures in the processes of institutional change.

Relationships and Social Structure

The point that society shapes attention pathways and proclivities leads us to another aspect of social cognition theory. While people can learn directly from mass media, they seek additional observations, including more personal ones, particularly when the new actions involve high costs and risk (Watt and van den Berg 1978), as in real estate development. The nature of the relationship between agents affects the kind of interactions they have and how they communicate, and these relationships vary among cultures. For example, depending on the society, parents may teach their children using verbal or nonverbal communication and relate to their children as peers or as mentors (Rogoff 1990). Similarly, the school of "communities of practice" emphasizes that learning new models is a social phenomenon because knowledge is specific to a community (Lave and Wenger 1991). Such theories follow along the lines of Vygotzky who proposed over a hundred years ago that society not only teaches people what to think but *how* to think (Vygotsky 1978).

The economic sociology and political economy literatures are especially helpful in illuminating the way society's structure impacts information flows. For example, ideas are generated and flow faster in a society characterized by weak social ties. If a society is structured predominantly by close-knit relationships, people will have less exposure to new ideas and will not spread them very quickly (Granovetter 1983). Similarly, power in hierarchical social structures may work to discourage negative feedback from people lower in the hierarchy, and it may limit innovation and learning in the upper echelons. This relationship requires a more nuanced understanding, however, when one considers that some authoritarian and hierarchical societies have also transitioned very quickly to capitalism.

The role of power and how it is organized in society is central to political science. The findings made it abundantly clear that political connections were very important to all of the firms. Without these connections, they would have no way to access the information and approvals needed to develop urban land in HCMC. More fundamentally, the connections also played a role in how people understood and thought about what their new roles in the economy were and what they could and could not do. As we have seen, political elites did not simply form firms by themselves and siphon off state assets. Rather, they needed to connect with people who had construction experience and other cultural capital. The firms then needed to find ways to collect advances from the public and to secure enough assurances of development rights before the official approval by the Prime Minister. They also had to learn how to run their businesses, knowledge that they gained from experience and through observing and sharing information with others.

The developers had to learn new paradigms and behavior. One place where I found that learning was *not* happening was in Vietnam's international development training programs. I sat in classrooms in Hanoi observing Swedes trying to teach Vietnamese civil servants how private real estate markets work. The history of development work by Sweden in Vietnam is admirable in its long-term and in-country commitment. Even so, as with most other development agencies, teaching duties were subcontracted to people who had limited experience with Vietnam's institutional context. The course material's disconnect with the local context was epitomized by the unabashed newspaper-reading by participants in the middle of the seminars. Another American colleague recounted that after lecturing at a similar training seminar in the Ukraine, he was finally asked by the civil servants what formulas they should use to set market prices. Meanwhile, outside of the classrooms, real estate markets grew rapidly without the benefit of lectures.

Another idea of the way people learn new behaviors is the concept of learning by doing. People try some actions, see the results, and refine their subsequent attempts, making improved decisions along the way. But the evolutionary process of trial and error assumes a type of tedious behavior in invoking simple-minded and unimaginative agents (Bandura 1997). It does not explain well the rapid and discontinuous social change we have seen in HCMC. According to the rational actor model, we would expect agents to make calculated decisions to engage in wholly new behavior. But developers' accounts do not conform to this narrative either. When asked how they first started developing land privately, the developers and other agents in the industry do not recount recognizing and deliberately seizing opportunities. Rather, they tell stories about how they fell into real estate development through a series of unintentional events and encounters with people they happened to meet along the way. Only with time did any of them conceptualize the system and the roles involved and identify themselves as developers. Eventually, they calculated the factors that would maximize their net profits. Adopting the orientation and role of private real estate developer was not innate but learned. The idea that people need to learn new economic behaviors is not novel. But its implications for international development and for scholarly thinking have not been adequately explored. In particular, the international development policy world, with its increasing reliance on market mechanisms, assumes that capitalistic behavior is natural.

The Centrality of Cognition in Institutional Change

The above presentation of the relevant cognitive literature about learning new behaviors has led us to the position that cognition is not just an individual matter but a social phenomenon. This recognition helps bridge the agent-versus-structure divide. As chapter 4 concluded, it was not only the individual entrepreneurs who changed their way of thinking. They were able to become the new phenomenon of private land developers in HCMC because a society-wide cognitive shift occurred that enabled the private firms and housing industry to emerge in HCMC.

Changes in economic relations are institutionalized when they can be conceived, actions typified, and interacted with predictably and habitually (Berger and Luckman 1967). Conversely, when something unpredictable and atypical happens, it causes surprise: one would say that is not what the institution is supposed to be or do. In HCMC, for example, the role of the developer recently became institutionalized in a society where it did not exist ten years earlier. Ordinary people now recognize developers as an entity, and they know that developers build and sell housing and residential plots. Similarly, government bureaucrats now know they can extract the development of public infrastructure from them. And farmers know that while developers may take the land they occupy and make a profit, they are able to negotiate for more compensation. The conception may shift depending on the corresponding agent, but the reciprocity of roles makes it social—together the agents reify the system. The emergence of Vietnamese capitalism entailed a major reconstruction of social cognition—a socially shared conception of the economy (see figure 5.1).

In other words, the fiscal socialism system is not an individual's perception nor was it designed by the state. The paradigm that is practiced does not exist in Vietnam's policies or in textbooks. Rather, it exists in the social cognitive realm—a specific and shared understanding of new economic relations, boundaries of behavior, and roles. Fiscal socialism was constructed through decentralized acts and debates. And this particular

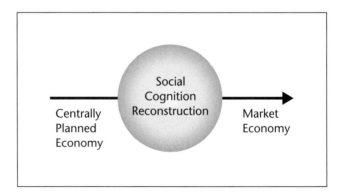

Figure 5.1 The centrality of social cognition in international development.

Vietnamese brand of capitalism which defies conventional wisdom required the construction of a shared understanding about
new economic roles in its society. This knowledge distinguished
the new capitalists from lay builders. But beyond changes in the
developers themselves, a social, cognitive change had to happen
in the rest of society in order for developers to be able to engage
in the interactions that would bring about these new actions.

The key change in fiscal socialism is that local governments
began negotiating with emerging private land developers to
exchange land rights for infrastructure development. This private negotiation could not occur at the national level because
it would threaten the state's legitimizing claim of serving the
public interest with its land management. But the transaction
between the developers and local government also could not
happen unless local society in HCMC literally started buying
into it. It was necessary for society to grapple with the tensions
and reconstruct the terms under which this transfer could take
place and the way it would be operationalized. The very material transfers of land could not have happened without this
reconstruction of social cognition.

The Old Paradigm

To appreciate the fundamental change in social cognition and
institutions that occurred, we need to take a moment to review
what housing provision looked like before Vietnam's transition.
In the centrally planned economy, land was not a commodity
but an administratively allocated resource. Enterprises would
request land for their operations from the state. Hence land did
not have location value as it does in a market economy, and cities did not exhibit the land use patterns typical of market cities
(Bertaud and Renaud 1995). Urban housing policy was formed
at the national level, and public housing projects were planned
and implemented by the lower levels of government. Officially,
housing in the old system was an entitlement, part of the state
welfare policy. A person had little choice about location since it
was connected to his assigned working unit. Households did

not have much mobility, as items such as their food were also tied to their household registration. In practice, however, the northern cities received more of the public housing projects, leaving the majority of HCMC residents to fend for themselves in declining housing conditions (Luan et al. 2000). Housing was often self-built, particularly in the rural areas, and informal transactions occurred before the transition even though public housing was the only official source of new housing.

The disparity between the official and the practiced was a common characteristic of Vietnamese communism. In particular, lower levels of government exercised considerable discretion in implementing the central government's plans. The literature has characterized Vietnamese local government behavior as ranging from rent-seeking to entrepreneurism to benevolent pragmatism (Leaf and Vinh 1996; Fforde and de Vylder 1996; Gainsborough 2003). The practice of unofficial local government discretion is one of the important factors contributing to Vietnam's, and in particular HCMC's, market transition.

In any case, fundamental changes in the economy occurred rapidly in Vietnam. When the government introduced the *doi moi* renovation policies in 1986, the economy began to liberalize with the transition. With state support, Vietnam dramatically increased its agricultural production through decollectivization, emerging as a net exporter of commodities such as rice by 1989 (Pingali and Xuan 1992). With economic growth, people could purchase goods instead of receive them, and thus they were no longer tied to their assigned residence. This change set off a huge demographic shift to the urban areas, where the population sought other educational and employment opportunities. In HCMC, the population increased by over one million between 1989 and 1999. In addition, incomes started to rise dramatically, particularly in HCMC, where the median household income doubled between 1990 and 1996 (HCMC Statistical Yearbook 1997). These changes fueled the demand for more housing and more housing options. The increased demand also strained the infrastructure and public services of the city, a need the local governments could not meet.

By the early 1990s, the vast majority of annual new housing supply was privately supplied in HCMC. Seven years after
the Land Law allowed the existence and sale of private property, one of my case firms estimated that the residential market in 2000 was worth around 4.4 trillion VND, or roughly $300
million USD. Much of the new housing represented individual
household coping strategies. But firms produced a significant
and growing portion of the private supply—roughly one-quarter
of private construction by the late 1990s (JBIC 1999). Key informants estimate that by the year 2000, there were roughly 200 private real estate and land development firms licensed in HCMC.

The Conventional Paradigm

Now that we have seen how housing and residential land used
to be delivered and managed, we can appreciate the significance
and breadth of the changes that occurred in HCMC's economy.
Many people shifted to new roles and relationships simultaneously. It is also significant that the fiscal socialism system is different from how residential land is supposed to be delivered in
a private real estate market. The atypical nature of HCMC's real
estate market has been documented by international private
real estate professionals. Because of Vietnam's slow changes in
legal institutions and the ad hoc approach to regulation and
taxation by local authorities, Jones Lang Lasalle's assessment
of global real investment climates ranked Vietnam dead last
on their list of 56 countries (Jones Lang LaSalle 2006). Other
international development agency land policy experts have also
pointed to Vietnam's lack of private property rights protection
as one of the key barriers to its economic development (UNDP
1995; Dang and Palmkvist 2001; Gillespie 2001). Interestingly,
however, Asian investors from Japan, Taiwan, and South Korea
began investing heavily early in Vietnam's transition, including
in the real estate sector.

Figure 5.2 illustrates how real estate markets are supposed to
work according to the conventional framework. Land development is conceived of as a series of discrete events occurring in a

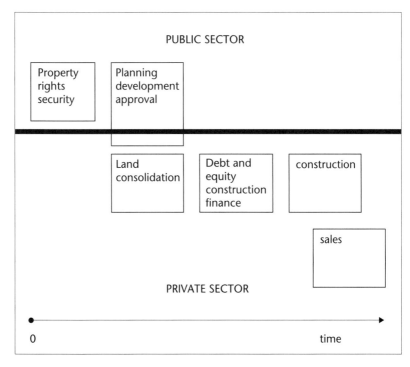

Figure 5.2 Conventional Paradigm of Real Estate Project Development.

linear progression over time. When countries began to make the transition to a private real estate market, international experts emphasized the need for building legal protections around private property rights. Recommended reforms revolved around three components: legal amendments, property title registration in modernized cadastral systems, and the court resolution of disputes (UNECE 1997). Legally protected private property rights were seen as a prerequisite for an efficiently operating real estate market and the lack of them one of the major reasons why some transition countries were having difficulty activating housing markets (CELK Center 2004).

The thinking was that private property rights must be secure because a firm will not be willing to invest in property that it is not able to keep. Part of this security means that the state must have clear boundaries on its expropriation powers and reasonable compensation for expropriation. In the conventional paradigm, the state and firms should have limited interaction, represented by the heavy line in figure 5.2. The state's primary role in the housing sector should be the provision and enforcement of laws and regulations. Within this framework, the firm begins to assemble land parcels for a project, usually as a series of private transactions without any state involvement.

The main direct interaction between the firm and state bureaus in the idealized scenario is in the processing of development approval from planning authorities. This is doubly critical because firms must secure planning and investment approval before they can receive bank loans—often a significant source of construction financing in developed countries—to pay for their new development. After planning approval is received and most of the financing is secured, construction may begin. Customers may also buy into the project during construction, but they are willing to do so because their rights are protected by contracts that are enforceable in courts.

Obviously, there are large differences between what actually happens in HCMC and the ideal scenario.[3] In particular, the market seems to tolerate insecure property rights. The state not only owns all land but is involved in every official transaction between two private parties. When developers buy land parcels to consolidate a project site, the land transactions require the intermediary step of returning the land back to the state. The Vietnamese state has strong powers of expropriation, which it has used. Developers and customers are investing into a project before they can receive official title to property. Meanwhile, most of the construction financing is coming from customers rather than from banks.

New Social Cognition Theory

In my earlier discussion of fiscal socialism in chapter 4, I outlined the interests that would be served by the new alignment of social economic relations. But the mystery is not that interests could be better served by an institutional change; in developing countries, there are many instances where mutual benefits and greater efficiency could be realized by social change. But too often, significant institutional change still does not happen. The question is, How does society go about changing? How did people in HCMC turn from being recipients of housing to being willing to hand over savings to new entities years before they saw their house? How did bureaucrats change from administering central government policies to negotiating deals with private firms? How did other people transform themselves from employees to being entrepreneurs? These changes are predicated on new ideas and conceptions—a reconstruction of economic relations and social facts. Yet most policymakers and many scholars assume away or ignore the cognitive realm of the economy.

Many studies of institutional change presume a fixed behavioral model and universal symbolic meanings. A conventional explanation for the entrepreneurial activity of HCMC real estate developers would be that an external change, the huge housing demand, altered the structure of their incentives and opportunities such that their new entrepreneurial actions would better serve their personal gain. But while housing shortages exist in many places in the world, an industry of private housing development firms does not necessarily grow rapidly as a result. As we saw in the beginning of the book, producing a desired economic behavior, such as investment and entrepreneurialism in real estate, is more difficult to engineer in practice than in theory. Some countries that followed the conventional policies to unleash the market stagnated, while some transition countries that did not follow the conventional policies, such as Vietnam, had tremendous growth and investment despite seemingly untenable risks. We are missing a major factor needed to explain the variation in economic transition outcomes.

This missing factor is cognition. Developmental psychologists have produced a rich literature that explores the way human mental processes mediate between environment and individual actions. Figure 5.3 outlines a new social cognition model of institutional change, building on Bandura's original social cognition model (1986) but incorporating the influence of power dynamics in society. The conventional institutional change framework deals only with the area under the dashed line: agents respond to changing macroeconomic conditions in their environment with new behavior. Therefore, policies can be designed to alter the external environment, which will alter the incentives in a human behavioral model that does not change and thereby produce a corresponding change in economic actions. The conventional models do have a feedback loop in which behaviors might create a demand for a change in the economic environment. Economists often represent institutions such as property rights with this bidirectional relationship between environment and behavior (Demsetz 1967).

In the truncated model, both the environment and behavior can change, but the cognitive model does not change. This model might adequately represent cases of institutional stasis where actions reify existing structures. Or, in structuralist parlance, agent cognition is so thickly structured by the environment that agents not only produce predictable actions, but they have little imagination for anything except the status quo. As discussed earlier, cognitive science has also shown that people will notice and more easily recall information that further confirms existing cognitive frameworks and discount or incorrectly recall information that does not. Again, this model works well for explaining existing and persisting institutional structures and actions that are beneath the dotted line in figure 5.3.

However, scholars are increasingly recognizing the need to reexamine cognitive processes in order to account for such things as the varieties of capitalism and the processes of economic change. In cases of major institutional change, old cognitive frameworks are challenged and reconstructed, leading to new behaviors and actions. DiMaggio (1997) refers to these circumstances as opportunities for reflective cognitive processes, as opposed to the automatic cognitive processes that occur under the dotted line in figure 5.3 in situations of institutional stasis. In instances where people change their own behavior, agents

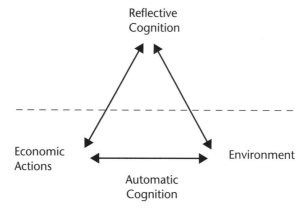

Figure 5.3 New social cognition model of institutional change.

undergo a more deliberative cognitive process. These occurrences are not as common, but when they do occur they involve cognitive processes involving attention to new information and vicarious learning from observing others.[4]

Chapter 3 detailed the variety of ways that the entrepreneurs found to develop projects and how these were shaped by social networks and social structure. The entrepreneurs' information-gathering process was facilitated by the availability of intermediaries and the openness of social networks. They paid a great deal of attention to the investment activities of politically powerful people in society when making their own project decisions in HCMC.

Within these general processes of learning, we observed a variety of approaches the entrepreneurs used to complete the four key development steps. Zerubavel explains that this is the case because the modern world is characterized by plural cognitive communities (1997). While agents do not invent their cognitive constructs, they may have considerable variation and some choice in the particular constellation of cognitive communities to which they belong and pay attention. Moreover, a particular society's structure may facilitate the ease of adopting a greater number and wider array of cognitive communities. So although firms might be located in similar social positions and have similar political privileges, they could still make some choices that affected how successful they were. Thus in the new social cognition model, society shapes agent cognition but not with homogeneous, deterministic outcomes. Institutional variation arises because people do not react to every influence or schema they confront in their environment. This dynamic is obvious in unsuccessful international development projects that produce little behavioral impact. In fact, in the face of many competing influences, people often display regular patterns of behavior that do not change easily. A person's environment does not dictate behavior except in the most coercive of situations.

The social cognition model shows us that significant changes in economic practices and economic institutions do not happen unless social cognition is engaged, because "institutions" are also internal, mental constructs rather than simply external entities. That is the key difference between institutions that have force and meaning and those that are formally declared but ignored in practice. For example, the Vietnamese market described earlier is what actually happens as opposed to what is supposed to happen according to laws and conventional wisdom. It arose as developers, various levels of government, home buyers, and farmers observed and negotiated with each other in redefining the terms of their relationship. While thick structuralists would debate how much choice people have, we need a better accounting of the institutional variety we observe and the lack of impact some structural interests have.

Social cognition's implication for social scientists is that the universality of human physiology cannot predict economic behavior. Much of neuroscience research examines the universal processes of human cognition related to physiological development and structure. Humans have advanced neural systems that are specialized for channeling attention, detecting causal structures in one's environment, processing that information into abstract form, and adapting behavior accordingly. This process is more commonly called learning and memory. Within the possibilities and limitations of our physiology, a wide range of adaptive behavior is evident in the empirical world. Human cognition is characterized by great plasticity.

The cognitive psychology of the 1960s emerged as a critique of postwar behaviorist models, which studied behavior apart from internal mental states. Beliefs were considered illusory, or at least not susceptible to analysis, and therefore the stimuli and resulting behavior mattered most (Skinner 1953). In contrast, the Piagetian approach emphasized the adaptability of our cognition and methods of constructing meaning and knowledge to order our world.

Cross-cultural research in cognitive development, however, has provided evidence that there are few universal psychological processes, in part because human development is so intimately tied to how societies make meaning of their world in a particular historical place and time (Rogoff 1990). A serious limitation of behaviorist research is that it tries to isolate variables through an experimental setting, but the experimental subjects (and the researcher!) bring with them heavily socialized constructs that have been internalized and cannot be left at the door of the laboratory.

Social and developmental psychology examines socially situated cognition, as opposed to either the behavioral idiosyncrasies of individual persons or cognitive universalism (Zerubavel 1997). Society shapes our use of physiological processes and interprets and attaches meaning to them, ultimately shaping our behavior and actions. A new approach in social science, still in the minority but growing (in such disciplines as cross-cultural psychology, social psychology, cultural anthropology, and cognitive sociology), is exploring how society interacts with agent cognition to produce the incredible variation we witness in behaviors and institutions.

This idea is particularly relevant since economic actions are not individual actions so much as interactions and transactions between agents. Therefore, this study presents the social construction of agents' intersubjectivity—the nonobjective, but suprapersonal "facts." Through the use of language, ideas and thoughts can be conveyed to others, implying that individual agent cognitions can be constituted by more than one's own personal experiences. Concepts can also be conveyed tacitly, by example rather than through verbal language. Through social interaction, we build up a host of shared understandings. The changes in social cognition that are fundamental to institutional change are not the original constructs of individuals. But because they are socially shared, it is also possible to locate the new constructs embedded in agents by examining the narratives repeated in society (Garfinkel 1967).

In sum, the new social cognition model shows that institutional change requires a dynamic model. The approach of eliciting new actions from individuals, who are confined to a static behavioral model, through a reengineering of their environment might be sufficient in situations of institutional stasis. But for major institutional changes, cognition must be reformulated socially.

In order to explain how a unique version of a private real estate market emerged in HCMC, this chapter has made the case that rather than assuming a static and universal behavioral model, we must examine these social cognitive processes. Cognitive paradigms shifted through dynamic interaction with the structural forces of the state, norms, and social protests and through the developers' learning from their new actions, from one another, and from other agents in society. Rather than innately knowing and deciding what to do, they were socialized into entrepreneurship.

The next chapter tests the general applicability of a social cognition perspective by examining transition-era Hanoi, where private firms did not emerge, and the emergence of private land developers in Poland and China.

Notes

1. Bandura's more recent work emphasizes that this learning process is dependent on instilling efficacy, the belief that one can do, in order to persevere through obstacles and setbacks. Self-efficacy is raised by seeing others similar to oneself succeed by sustained effort (Bandura 1997).

2. Some argue that Vietnam and China looked more to the developmental state model of the East Asian miracle economies than to the Western paradigm in the beginning of transition. As Japan and Korea experienced economic woes during the 1990s, however, they had to look for another approach (Perkins 2001).

3. In fact, most of the developing world does not follow this ideal, but, as in Vietnam, has an inverted progression with the disbursal of land title being the final act rather than the prerequisite (Pamuk 1996). Transition cases such as Vietnam, however, are also different from typical developing country cases in the level of state involvement in the private sector.

4. Neuroscience research has shown that different areas of the brain and different frequency channels occur with different kinds of attention. Attention to external stimuli occurs in the posterior parietal cortex, whereas willful modes of attention engage the prefrontal cortex (Buschman and Miller 2007).

6

Comparisons with Other Transition Economies

Social cognition provides a more general framework for understanding the process of institutional change and helps explain
why Ho Chi Minh City developed its particular variety of capitalism. Our investigation into the rapid transition that occurred
in HCMC showed that while incentives and interests may
be aligned, a social cognitive phenomenon also needs to be
engaged. People in society must also be able to collectively create new roles in the economy, negotiating their new terms and
boundaries. As people pay attention to and observe one another,
the possibility of new roles and boundaries spreads and are
contested. As the socially constructed knowledge disseminates
and leads to predictable patterns of behavior, a new social reality is created and real institutional change has occurred. As we
have seen, in HCMC the outcome of this social construction
project depended on both the particular alignment of society's
interests as well as the way society's structure shaped the pathways of attention, learning, and cultural resources that could
be redeployed in supporting new ideas, behaviors, and roles.
These processes all played an instrumental role in developing
HCMC's fiscal socialism.

If the social cognition framework is valuable, it should also help to better explain other transition cases. At the outset of this book, I observed that the variation among the transition countries creates a puzzle. There were places like Vietnam that transitioned quickly despite not following the conventional set of institutional reforms, while other transition cases that did follow conventional reforms produced mixed results, with some growing steadily and others making little progress. These outcomes suggest the limited efficacy of a policy strategy based on institutional universals.

In this chapter I will examine whether the new social cognition theory can provide insight into the puzzle through an analytically useful combination of comparative cases. Hanoi, Vietnam's capital city, had the same macroeconomic conditions and policy strategies as HCMC, but few private land development firms emerged there. Warsaw, Poland, is a case that has been held up as an exemplar of the conventional reforms, but, as we will see, an investigation of the private firms themselves reveals many surprising similarities to, and important differences from, the emergence and operation of HCMC firms. Finally, I will make some comparative observations based on the findings from the outpouring of research on China's urban transition; these, again, will show that there are significant similarities to, as well as differences from, transition-era HCMC. These comparisons will help illuminate the social cognition process in other societies and the essentials of the transition process. Comparative analysis also provides further insights into why HCMC was able to transition so rapidly.

The Lack of Entrepreneurs in Hanoi

Firms did not emerge in Hanoi as they did in HCMC, even though both cities have the same basic legal and governmental framework, transition policies, and high market demand. Why wouldn't people in Hanoi form land development firms and try to take advantage of the great profits that could be made?

While the formal laws and government structure are identical throughout the whole nation, no researcher in Vietnam can escape the oft-mentioned stereotypes about differences between northerners and southerners. With the north's history as the epicenter of the Communist revolution and state power, some portray northerners as more rigid about regulations and more hostile to private business (Dapice et al. 2004). Differences in the two cities' real estate markets are not surprising, given the way Vietnam's political history affected local land management institutions. During the French colonial period, the south had established private property registers by the 1890s (Wiegersma 1988). During the 1950s, before the revolution, land tenure varied greatly between Vietnam's three major regions, with the south having many absentee landlords, central Vietnam having more communal land ownership, and the north pursuing five waves of land reform, expropriating land from nearly 58% of the population (Moise 1983).

Others dwell less on the pre-Communist past and point to current differences between the two cities' local governments. Some see HCMC's government leaders as being in the vanguard of Vietnam's reform (Turley and Womack 1998) out of the sheer economic necessity of coping with a central government that has historically given a disproportionate share of transfers to the northern regions. Others have concluded that northern city bureaucrats simply lack the ability to work productively with private business (Dapice et al. 2004). But still others take issue with this characterization, pointing out that government bureaus and elites in HCMC have also exhibited predatory actions toward business, just as in the rest of the country (Gainsborough 2003).

My research suggests that there *are* significant differences in the political economies of Hanoi and HCMC. According to HCMC-based real estate development firms that investigated setting up shop in the north, Hanoi does not provide comparable open entry into the market. Although exact figures are not available, one developer estimates that in HCMC the state directly controls land development for about 30% of the parcels and 50% of the developable land area, whereas in Hanoi it controls 90% of the parcels and almost all of the land area. But the paucity of private firms in Hanoi provides the most striking evidence that land supply and development are overwhelmingly dominated by political elites and state-owned companies. From the viewpoint of neoclassical economics, Hanoi's housing shortage should provide more than enough incentive for private firms to form in the north because the profit margins would be large (Dowall and Landis 1982), but Hanoi's oligarchy dominates market share through control of land supply. And, as we will see, an analysis of market data shows that Hanoi's housing market has higher prices and crowding as a result of these supply-side constraints.

One of my case firms, Firm #4, was able to develop one workers' housing project in Hanoi, although most of its operations are in the south. The leader recounted that one needs much more powerful friends to be able to work in Hanoi than in HCMC. The Hanoi city government required his firm to contribute 30% of the developed units at cost. Because of this requirement, the government audits firm operations very carefully, in order to calculate the lowest cost. To make the project feasible, the firm had to work with state- or city-owned companies as subcontractors and had to have good relations with the director of the Office for Prices to be able to get a higher selling price. Firm #6 originated in Hanoi with a staff of northerners, but it ended up moving its operations to the south. While it had good political connections, the firm also stated that Hanoi is a much more difficult place to do business, requiring exceptional relationships with people in the central government ministries. The closed networks in Hanoi are a major difference from HCMC. Hundreds of private land and housing development firms formed in HCMC within the first decade of transition (JBIC 1999). Despite its being imperfectly competitive, the entrepreneurs I interviewed confirmed open entry into the market, using their own personal histories of how they started in the business as an example.

One reason that HCMC's government has interacted more amenably with private business is that it desperately needed other sources of public finance. Its population grew by more than a million people in less than a decade while transfers from the central government did not increase proportionally. The housing shortage was exacerbated by the fact that more of the limited amount of public housing investments from 1975 to 1985 ended up going to state employees in northern cities (Luan et al. 2000).

While it is true that the Communist Party appoints the highest positions in city government in HCMC, southerners often make up the rest of the staff. The bureaucracy in HCMC has often been considered relatively more pragmatic (Turley and Womack 1998), and it started going off-plan before *doi moi* (Fforde and Luong 1996). The south often initiates bureaucratic innovations. For example, some of HCMC's districts experimented with pilot programs, such as the one-stop office to organize and expedite procedures for obtaining land development permits, sparing applicants a lengthy trek through a maze of bureaus. While this experiment did not succeed as planned (Gainsborough 2002a), it still shows a greater openness to administrative reform experiments.

But my informants pointed to other reasons for the two cities' differences in entrepreneurship. As one private real estate developer remarked, "The biggest difference between the north and south is social perception…in the south you may tax profits but the attitude is 'Good for you!' whereas in the north they have a criminal atmosphere." These differences in attitudes also affected the social norms about property rights. Social norms are cultural constructs that have some teeth to them because they are enforced by social sanctions (Posner and Rasmusen 1999). In the previous chapters' investigations of how HCMC's private housing industry functions, we observed a loose attitude toward property rights and legal documentation. Not only did entrepreneurs willingly invest in property before they received official government approvals, but the district governments also encouraged this practice. Furthermore, customers were willing to pay for a house on the basis of a site plan drawing and a private contract, sometimes years before the ground was broken.

Although courts could not enforce such contracts, people were confident that they were sufficient.[1] In HCMC's fiscal socialism, the title for the property and development approval often came after the fact, assisted by the looseness and flexibility of the city's property rights norms.

The purportedly more rigid norms about property, profit, and regulations in the north imply that the kind of fiscal socialism that developed in HCMC would not be possible in Hanoi because each of the parties involved would not be willing to transact easily outside of the regulations and without legal documentation. If true, this situation would partly explain why we see so few private land development firms in Hanoi. During the times I lived in Vietnam, I often heard people speak about these differences. Southerners who had traveled, lived, or worked in Hanoi often told me how difficult it was for them to conduct economic transactions there. Hanoians would not negotiate easily, and they seemed more meticulous and exacting about documentation and following regulations. It was easy for the comments to devolve into stereotypes that scholars do not like to propagate.

We have still another way to examine the differences in property norms between the two regions. Hedonic price models can be used to show how people in Hanoi and HCMC value ambiguity in property rights status. Rather than asking for opinions, we can use market data to determine what kind of price patterns emerge for properties that have and do not have title in each of these cities. With this data we can test the hypothesis that Hanoi has significantly more rigid social norms about legal, documented property rights.

The statistical analysis does not imply that norms about property somehow trump the explanatory power of political interests in accounting for the different economic outcomes of Hanoi and HCMC. It is important to note that norms about property and the structure of the two cities' political economies are interrelated. On the one hand, property norms will be embedded in the agents who are dealing with property transactions. On the other hand, the norms will reflect the local political economy and the reality of the ways in which sanctions are structured and meted. The point here, however, is not to dissect this interrelationship but to find evidence of significant differences between the two cities in how people operationalized their property rights in ways that impacted the ability of private firms to emerge. Even though these house sellers live in the same country, they have internalized different local norms about how to value their claim to property, which in effect expresses and serves to support the particular local political economy.

Property Rights Institutions in Theory and Practice

The 1993 Land Law allowed private persons or entities land use rights that they could possess, transfer and mortgage. While the state retained ownership, the official commodification of land condoned the rise of private housing markets. While private land development firms did not flourish in Hanoi, in both Hanoi and HCMC private transactions between households proliferated, which helped to relieve the housing shortages. In both cities, many of these real estate transactions did not perfectly conform to all the regulations. In particular, at that time urban households were required to obtain a Building Ownership and Land Use Certificate (BOLUC), which combines home ownership with the land use right into one legal document. Also known as "the pink certificate" for its color, the BOLUC provided the equivalent to having a fully titled private residential property. Between its introduction and 2001, however, less than 25% of all Vietnamese households had obtained them (Dang and Palmkvist 2001).[2] There are many reasons for the lack of title distribution, including missing supporting documents, lingering property disputes contesting ownership, inadequate administrative capacity of the wards and districts to help process the title, and the disincentive of tax liabilities.

The pink certificates were not necessary for homeowners to effectively prove their property right and exchange it because

they could use a variety of alternative property rights enforcement mechanisms. Enforcement institutions are an important
issue, since property claims are only truly rights if they are
enforced (Cole and Grossman 2002), and thus the outcome of
dispute resolution provides the true test of a claim's status as
a right. Like other centrally planned countries, Vietnam has an
elaborate government bureaucracy involved in many aspects of
household economic life. Compared to other Communist states
in Asia, however, Vietnam is characterized by a high degree
of discretion at the lower levels of government (Fforde and de
Vylder 1996; Leaf and Vinh 1996; Gainsborough 2002b).

For example, in HCMC, the majority of land and housing
disputes are handled by neighborhood communities and local
bureaucrats (see figure 6.1). The first and lowest institution for
handling many kinds of disputes is the residential block commit-
tees, the *to dan pho*. Outsiders are often surprised by the extent
to which neighbors in Vietnam can weigh in on what would be
deemed private household affairs in other contexts. But the moti-
vation is to resolve disputes locally and as quickly as possible
through arbitration in order to avoid more official involvement
of higher levels of government. If the *to dan pho* cannot resolve
a dispute, the ward may get involved. Many ward offices desig-
nate bureaucrats to deal exclusively with land and housing issues
in their ward. Ward officials in HCMC estimate that 30–50% of
the cases they hear annually concern land and housing issues
and that they can resolve roughly 70% of them. The ward officers often have more detailed information about local disputants
because they have not only their own records but their own social
networks and relationships with the residents as well. Disputes
unresolved at the ward level of government may gain a hearing
with the district government's land and housing departments
and civil courts. In the late 1990s, district courts in HCMC heard
about 600 housing cases a year, and approximately one-third of
these were referred on appeal to city courts; these took an average of one to three years to be resolved (Gillespie 1999).

While similar data are unavailable for Hanoi, government
officials in the land law field confirm that neighborhood block

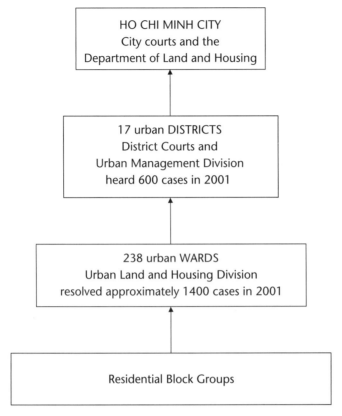

Figure 6.1 Property rights enforcement institutions in practice in HCMC, 2001.

groups and ward governments arbitrate many cases in Hanoi as well. Thus, in Vietnam one can have state-sanctioned property rights that are not necessarily enforced by the courts and property registers, the institutions that are the focus of international development projects. Other studies in Asia also suggest that property rights enforcement and dispute resolution may be administered through existing state organizations that may not have been formally assigned the duty by law but effectively enforce them (Leaf 1994; Gillespie 1999).

In sum, most property rights disputes in Vietnam are settled and enforced by neighbors and ward and district governments.

These institutions can exercise a great deal of discretion in the way they handle property rights enforcement (Leaf and Vinh 1996). For example, it is common for wards to stamp property transactions for parcels that do not have title. Furthermore, we have already observed that HCMC has a long tradition of local government operating outside of the central government's plan. This room for discretion allows for variation in how property rights are enforced between regions in Vietnam. So if the norm in the north is to follow the letter of the law more closely, we would expect that in cases of dispute, neighbors and local bureaucrats would side more with those who had the latest official documents, such as a pink certificate, and possibly penalize those who transacted without it. In comparison, with HCMC's loose social norms about legal documentation in proving property rights, we would expect greater leniency in the kinds of documents that would provide property rights enforcement.

Property Norms in Hanoi and Ho Chi Minh City

When I lived in Vietnam, I noticed a rapid growth, in both Hanoi and HCMC, in the number of private newspaper advertisements taken by households wishing to sell their property. I was struck by the amount of information contained in these advertisements and especially by the frequent mention of property rights status. These ads would cite a variety of documents to confirm their property rights, ranging from the pink certificate to a variety of "legal papers." I realized that, in contrast to most developing countries that lack market information, these provided enough data for statistical analysis. Most of the ads identified the seller's ward, providing a small enough geographical unit to make location a variable that could be linked to city census data.[3]

I employed a hedonic price model to find the market value for different forms of property rights. Hedonic price models are multilinear regression models in which the variable coefficients predict a portion of the house's market value (Rosen 1974; Box and Cox 1964; Goodman and Kawai 1984). Other studies have used these models to show that housing markets in the developing world can distinguish and price the premium for legal tenure (Jimenez 1984; Dowall and Leaf 1991).

I conducted one study using issues of the newspaper *Tuoi Tre* for the years 1998–2001 to study changing market trends in HCMC (Kim 2004). Later, I used a classified-advertisement daily newspaper that published issues in both Hanoi and HCMC, *Mua va Ban* (literally, "Buy and Sell") (Kim 2007). I realized that developing models for both cities' markets provided a particularly useful research design to test the importance of local norms. The uniform legal and government administrative structure, as well as the high demand conditions in both markets, would hold many variables constant. I collected 5,162 observations from all of the issues in both cities between March and June 2004 to determine how each market might price varying levels of legal property rights (table 6.1).[4]

One of the most interesting aspects of the data is that the property rights terms commonly used by house sellers in Hanoi differ from those used in HCMC. By 2004 the sellers in HCMC most commonly referred to formal title as *Chu quyen hong* or "pink certificate." In an earlier study, vaguer terms such as "owner certificate" were more commonly used. In following the evolution of the terms used in these ads, I found an increase in the mention of property rights claims and variation in terms in HCMC. In any case, of the listed properties in HCMC, 69.1% of sellers claimed possession of the pink certificate. Meanwhile, Hanoians used a different term to refer to the same document: *so do*, which can be translated as "red certificate." Originally, housing ownership and land use rights entailed separate certificates, with the red certificates used for the latter. But the latest regulations required a pink certificate to combine house ownership and land use right into one document for urban areas, while the red certificate could still be used for agricultural land. The difference seems to exist primarily in language, as key informants confirmed that Hanoians refer to the pink BOLUC when they say "red certificate." Hanoians seem to be slower to adopt new terms. Also, unlike HCMC sellers, many

Table 6.1 Descriptive statistics of houses listed for sale in Hanoi and HCMC, 2004

	Hanoi					HCMC				
	n	median	SD	min	max	n	median	SD	min	max
Prices										
All Prices in millions VND/m²	1632	10	15.33	1.34	222	3541	9.43	10.92	0.68	175
House Characteristics										
number of stories	1864	3.0	1.40	1	6	3476	2.0	1.03	1	7
floor area (square meters)	1864	110.0	95.96	10	675	3541	90	90.00	11	672
distance to CBD (km)	1632	4	1.72	1	13	3541	5.17	2.54	1	16
Amenities (dummies)	*n*	*mean*	*SD*	*min*	*max*	*n*	*mean*	*SD*	*min*	*max*
street facing	132	0.071	0.257	0	1	677	0.191	0.393	0	1
water	1864	1.000	0.000	1	1	3439	0.971	0.167	0	1

electricity	1864	1.000	0.000	1	1	3541	1.000	0.000	1	1
telephone	1856	0.996	0.065	0	1	3388	0.957	0.202	0	1
toilet	1863	0.999	0.023	0	1	3541	1.000	0.000	1	1
proximity to market	67	0.036	0.186	0	1	668	0.189	0.391	0	1
proximity to school	22	0.012	0.108	0	1	580	0.164	0.370	0	1
Property Rights (dummies)										
Red/pink certificate	1139	0.611	0.488	0	1	2445	0.691	0.462	0	1
Waiting for red certificate	212	0.114	0.318	0	1	846	0.239	0.427	0	1
Legal papers	427	0.225	0.418	0	1					
Total *n*	1632					3541				
Ads mentioning property rights	1622					3482				

Source: Kim, Annette. 2007. North versus South: The Impact of Social Norms in the Market Pricing of Private Property Rights in Vietnam. *World Development* 35 (12): 2079–95.

sellers in Hanoi also use the term *cho so do*, which means they are "waiting for red certificate" after submitting their application. There could be a greater backlog in issuing BOLUCs in the north. Perhaps Saigonese are also looser in their claim of possessing the BOLUC while they are still waiting for its issuance. In any case, only in the north is the distinction so commonly made, again indicating a greater formal exactness with practices in Hanoi. We would expect to see some difference in the market value between those properties claiming BOLUC and those that are waiting for it.

There is one term that is commonly used in both cities. *Giay to hop le* is a vague phrase that, literally translated, means "papers in accordance to regulation," or more loosely, "legal papers." These papers include the variety of documents that can be used to apply for the pink certificate. Many variants of this term are used in the ads, referring to specific legal papers such as building permits, the old housing permits, and so forth; for the purposes of this study, all of these were grouped into a single "legal papers" category because the listers mention them as proof of ownership right even though the law accords them less standing than the pink certificate. Despite the differences in the scale of markets and histories, both cities' advertisements use this term with similar frequency: 22.5% in Hanoi, 23.9% in HCMC.

While economic factors such as large potential gains from skyrocketing demand can provide incentives for a systemic change in private property rights, the vocabularies for the new private property rights have evolved differently in the two markets: "pink certificate" and "ownership certificate" in the south and "red certificate" and "waiting for red certificate" in the north. These linguistic differences suggest different cultural perceptions about the law and property. The question is whether these linguistic differences also have economic significance. They should, since the BOLUC, or pink certificate, was the most recent and secure form of tenure. A pink certificate meant that the seller had invested time and money in obtaining the title, which should be reflected in the sales price. Certainly, transferring ownership of property with a pink certificate is easier, since the certificates are issued only if there are no outstanding property disputes.

Table 6.2 shows the result of the base models for Hanoi and HCMC. The models have a good fit with all the signs of the

Table 6.2   Comparison of base models

HCMC model Estimation method	Base model semi-log	Hanoi model Estimation method	Base model semi-log
Constant	5.073	Constant	5.746
Distance to CBD	−0.117	Distance to CBD	−0.012
	(−4.667)		(−0.317)
Floor area (m²)	0.537	Floor area (m²)	0.502
	(47.480)		(25.634)
Street facing house	0.251	Street facing house	0.306
	(22.260)		(16.787)
School	0.038	Telephone	0.041
	(3.444)		(2.281)
Percent housing quality high	0.116	Percent housing quality low	−0.110
	(6.254)		(−4.612)
Education rate high	0.078	Education rate high	0.114
	(3.781)		(4.600)
District dummies entered		*District dummies entered*	
CBD	0.023	CBD	−0.004
	(1.166)		(−0.141)
Urban fringe	0.031	Urban fringe	−0.081
	(0.509)		(−3.200)
Adjusted R^2	0.586	Adjusted R^2	0.467

Source: Kim, Annette. 2007. North versus South: The Impact of Social Norms in the Market Pricing of Private Property Rights in Vietnam. *World Development* 35 (12): 2079–95.

Notes: Dependent variable is *ln house prices* in Vietnamese dong (VND). Coefficients are standardized betas; *t*-statistics are indicated in parentheses. District Binh Chanh was excluded from the HCMC model, and District Dong Da was excluded from the Hanoi model. Observations entered: $n_1 = 3{,}537$, $n_2 = 1{,}631$.

variables in the expected direction. As in all normal property markets, prices generally fall the farther houses are located away from the city center and generally rise with more floor area, street frontage, and living amenities. The coefficients are also similar to those of the previous study of HCMC that used data from a different newspaper source, further indicating the robustness of the model (Kim 2004).

However, the explanatory power of the HCMC models, which have an R^2 of 0.586, is higher than for the Hanoi models with an R^2 of 0.467. Furthermore, in the Hanoi model, the variable that measures the distance from the city center is insignificant. A premium for being near downtown is one the characteristics we should observe in a city's real estate market that has transitioned away from a centrally planned economy (Bertaud and Bertrand 1995). For example, in HCMC's market house prices decrease by 11.7% with every kilometer away from the central business district (CBD).

We also find some other important differences between the two markets. One is that when city district dummy variables were entered in the Hanoi model to further account for a house's neighborhood value, only two of them were significant. In the HCMC model, however, most district variables were significant, commanding different premiums or liabilities even after holding other location variables constant, such as whether they were in the downtown area. HCMC's market values a property's location more sensitively than Hanoi's. The lower explanatory power of the Hanoi model and the insignificance of location variables suggest that Hanoi's housing market is still somewhat atypical in comparison with other markets. Hanoi's higher median housing prices and higher building densities (see table 6.1), coupled with Hanoi's lower median incomes, confirm the land supply-side constraints the private firms and key informants related.

The key variables of interest surround property rights. We have observed differences in the vocabularies lay people use in the two cities for property rights, despite a uniform legal

Table 6.3   Ho Chi Minh City property rights models

Model Estimation method	Model 1 semi-log	Model 2 semi-log	Model 3 semi-log
Constant	5.108	5.058	4.940
Distance to central business district	−0.118	−0.119	−0.120
	(−4.721)	(−4.772)	(−4.791)
Floor area of house (m²)	0.537	0.537	0.536
	(47.539)	(47.510)	(47.502)
Street	0.251	0.251	0.250
	(22.239)	(22.295)	(22.178)
School	0.039	0.038	0.039
	(3.581)	(3.511)	(3.555)
Housing quality high	0.116	0.117	0.116
	(6.264)	(6.298)	(6.256)
Education rate high	0.077	0.078	0.077
	(3.750)	(3.794)	(3.760)
District and location dummies entered	Yes	Yes	Yes
Pink certificate	.039	0.054	0.110
	(3.487)	(2.890)	(3.794)
Legal papers		0.019	0.070
		(1.040)	(2.556)
"Ownership certificate"			0.043
			(2.521)
Adjusted R^2	0.587	0.587	0.588

Source: Kim, Annette. 2007. North versus South: The Impact of Social Norms in the Market Pricing of Private Property Rights in Vietnam. *World Development* 35 (12): 2079–95.
Note: Coefficients are standardized betas; *t*-statistics are in parentheses; $n = 3{,}537$.

framework. Table 6.3 shows the results for HCMC, and table 6.4 shows the results for Hanoi.[5] As we would expect, both Hanoi and HCMC models show that the seller who explicitly states that he possesses the BOLUC (a pink or red certificate) can ask the highest offer price. Hanoians can ask for a 7% premium, while sellers in HCMC can demand about 11% more if they have already obtained the pink certificate.

Table 6.4 Hanoi property rights models

Model Estimation Method	Model 1 semi-log	Model 2 semi-log
Constant	5.758	5.799
Distance to central business district	−0.013	−0.010
	(−0.340)	(−0.277)
Floor area of house (m2)	0.482	0.481
	(24.762)	(24.813)
Street	0.302	0.301
	(16.789)	(16.799)
Telephone	0.035	0.033
	(1.950)	(1.830)
House quality low	−0.098	−0.096
	(−4.128)	(−4.061)
Education rate high	0.120	0.122
	(4.901)	(5.026)
District and location dummies entered	yes	yes
Red certificate	0.132	0.070
	(7.039)	(2.806)
Legal papers		−0.092
		(−3.776)
Adjusted R^2	0.483	0.487

Source: Kim, Annette. 2007. North versus South: The Impact of Social Norms in the Market Pricing of Private Property Rights in Vietnam. World Development 35 (12): 2079–95.
Note: Coefficients are standardized betas; t-stats in parentheses; n = 1,631.

The term "legal papers" has opposite effects in the two markets, however. In Hanoi, the possession of legal papers negatively affect offer prices. Sellers decrease their offer price by 9% if they mention these. Buyers and sellers must expect to transact with some proof of property right because nearly every advertisement does so and because otherwise no seller would advertise legal papers if it would lower his or her asking price. It appears that the Hanoian housing market is less tolerant of ambiguous property rights, and the seller has internalized it into his or her initial offer price. But HCMC is a different story. "Legal papers" is significantly positive and can still command a 7% premium over properties that do not advertise possession of any paper property rights. The term "legal papers" has a lower premium than "pink certificate," but it is still valued as something between being fully titled and having no documentation. In the south, it appears that "legal papers" are viewed as a midway property right rather than a lack of title.

The evidence presented here shows differences in how lay people in Hanoi and HCMC priced their property rights documentation. In both cases, they could command a premium for possessing the latest pink certificate. But if they did not possess it (and most households did not yet have it), Hanoi sellers lowered their offer price, whereas HCMC sellers still thought it had positive value in the marketplace, although not as great as having the pink certificate. In each case, the sellers are anticipating how potential buyers will react to their property rights documents. Their expectations reflect each city's social norms about property. When enforcing one's property rights in cases of dispute, Vietnamese would turn to their neighbors and local ward and district governments who practiced considerable discretion in these judgments. The statistical evidence lends support to the popular notion that northerners have a more exacting approach to following legal regulations, whereas southerners are more casual about legal documents.

This finding has rather devastating implications for international development. Although the same policies and legal reforms were applied in the same country, we see that it was not enough to initiate changes in Hanoi's private economic activity. Part of the challenge lies in the political interests holding back the land supply that entrepreneurs need for projects. But the related challenge is that their potential customers would also hold back from investing their savings into products without the legal documents. It is not surprising, then, that HCMC's fiscal socialism did not emerge in Hanoi. Even though, as noted by area specialists, bureaucrats practiced discretion in Hanoi as well as in HCMC, their interactions with others were within the boundaries of their local society. Both private citizens and local bureaucrats shared an understanding about property and economic transactions, and this understanding became a norm through social sanctions. Hanoi's social cognition made it more difficult to experiment and to form new relations and new actions outside of the regulations. The individuals in Hanoi who wanted to become private land developers eventually moved to the south, and the southern firms that tried to pursue projects in the north were stymied.

Unsociable Entrepreneurs in Warsaw, Poland

After my work in HCMC, I wanted to study a Central European transition case. After finding that capitalist institutions were socially constructed instead of naturally occurring, I wondered what had happened in the case of the poster children for successful economic transition. Were the reform policies really the reason for their rapid transition, or was social cognition an important aspect of their transitions as well?

Poland is an apt transition case to investigate not only because of its economic growth, but also because its property rights reforms have been touted as exemplary. The International Monetary Fund (2000) concluded that Poland had one of the best sets of pro-market institutions among 31 transition countries, and in particular the IMF lauded its ability to conduct small-scale privatization.[6] In fact, when in 2003 the Central European Land Knowledge (CELK) Center established the Regional Center of Excellence for Real Property Rights and Land Market Development in order to promote adequate real property rights legislation and monitoring, its mission statement refers to the property rights reforms of Poland, along with those of the Czech Republic and Hungary, as the role models for other Eastern European transition countries.

Warsaw's real estate industry experts have been tracking the trends in the housing market during the transition (REAS 2002; PMR Ltd. 2004; Szafarz 2003). The reports suggest that cooperatives played an important part from the early transition period until the private sector started to grow significantly in 1998. By 2003 the private sector dominated the annual production of housing. What accounts for the emergence of the private housing industry in Warsaw?

Since Vietnam and Poland differ in many important ways, I needed to get a sense of the historical and institutional differences as they related to land management. In particular, I wondered how Poland's pre-Communist and pre-transition conditions predisposed it to a private housing market and industry. As in HCMC, I also investigated how the agents in the housing development industry actually go about developing projects and the cognitive processes that informed their new economic actions. Poland might have an impressive institutional framework on paper, but, as I found in Vietnam, engaging the entrepreneurs directly could illuminate the need to reform theories.

My investigation in Warsaw represented a more limited study than my examination of HCMC. I spent less time in Poland, instead enlisting the help of a local colleague who had left academia and founded a real estate consultancy firm in Warsaw. He introduced me to six residential development firms for case study. The firms varied in their size and type, and this variation intriguingly corresponded to the types of firms found in HCMC (private, formerly state-owned, and foreign joint-venture). I also interviewed five additional key informants not linked to him and his company: two property lawyers, a representative from a title insurance company, and two Polish academics. Interviews with two commercial real estate consultants with residential development experience also helped to triangulate the findings.

As in HCMC, I asked the interviewees about their background, social group membership, and interactions with other firms in order to explore the questions about social networks and privilege. I asked a series of questions about their experience in developing each phase of their projects to identify their greatest challenges and how they overcame them. I also visited the firms' offices, reviewed their project designs and documents, and walked their project sites. The fieldwork for this study was conducted in April 2004.

All interviewees were unanimous about several features of private land development in Warsaw: securing site control was the most difficult step in developing projects, sub-city levels of government played an important role in facilitating development approval, legal documents were crucial, and there was little social networking between firms.

Despite major differences in initial conditions and reform paths, the operation of Warsaw's housing market has many striking similarities to HCMC's market. The interviewees unanimously pointed to securing project sites as the main risk and difficulty in developing housing projects in Warsaw. While land sellers on the periphery (which was agricultural land in the beginning of transition) usually had clear ownership, land negotiations were still difficult, in part because the payment to the seller depended on the cash flow from pre-sales of future units and on the government development approval process.

Poland has a long history of private land ownership. Over time, land parcels on the periphery became fragmented by inheritance subdivisions. To assemble a project site, a developer would often have to negotiate with 50 to 70 landowners. In order to avoid higher prices, firms would usually hire someone locally to surreptitiously buy parcels on their behalf. For the holdouts, they would either pay significantly higher prices or exclude the last parcel. More recently, some developers have begun buying land from non-agricultural investors who have already assembled parcels over the years. In either case, land sellers sign preliminary notarized contracts that firms use to secure the first development option and to transfer the right to the firm. Sellers willing to accept a lower price can receive a lump sum payment; otherwise, contracts specify an initial 10%

down payment followed by installment payments based on project completion stages.

The price that firms are willing to pay for land is based on estimates of the number of units they will be allowed to build and are able to sell. While firms await development approval, financing and economic conditions may change such that the firm or buyer will want to renegotiate the contract. The interviewees noted that they have been writing increasingly complex contracts. For example, contracts stipulate that the amount of future installment payments is subject to changes in the number of units approved by authorities, the size of units, and infrastructure costs. Meanwhile, the developers collect their project development capital through pre-sales of units, which also entail detailed contracts.

In practice, however, despite their increasing complexity, these contracts lack specificity, fostering conditions for disputes that are not easily enforced or resolved by courts. The firms often used generic "boilerplate" contracts with vaguely worded clauses that favor the developer. For example, in the sales contract the price of the apartment may be expressed as a price per square meter without specifying the total size of the unit, or it may be dependent on price indexing for increases in building materials costs but without giving details about which indices will be used. This ambiguity allows the developers to later change the prices for both buying the land and for selling developed units. Not surprisingly, nonprofessional parties tend to be disadvantaged in the process of negotiating contracts. As in HCMC, the firms strike a balance between the price of the presold units, which provide their development capital, and the price for the development option they bought from the farmer, which is a significant portion of their development costs, as they wait for development approval from the government.

Another major similarity with HCMC is that development authority was decentralized to sub-city levels of government, which had a great deal of autonomy. In 1990, constitutional revisions fundamentally reorganized the state. The administrative structure of Poland was realigned from 49 to 16 provinces, called *voivodships*. These were divided into self-governing *gminas*, or boroughs (Regulski 2003). In Warsaw, the central *gmina* was further subdivided into seven districts. The decentralization of authority was a different strategy than the one used in the Czech Republic, which concentrated power to an elite transition team in the central government. Because Poland's Solidarity labor movement had a strong network of grassroots organizations, the strategy was to increase local democracy to delegitimize and solidify the transition away from the Communist, centrally planned model and toward inclusion into the European Union (McDermott 2002).

Gminas were allowed to experiment with institutional reform and were involved in privatization and economic restructuring. As part of this decentralization effort, in the mid-1990s all land development authority was transferred to the *gminas*, which had their own councils, while other local government agencies still controlled some aspects of building permits and planning approvals. The administrative reform helped to cut the transaction costs for firms by reducing the number of special units involved in development projects. Firms could obtain approval for land development projects with a preliminary opinion from the *gmina* and start the project within a couple of months of submitting the application. The interviews suggest that the decentralization of development approval authority contributed significantly to the rapid takeoff of the housing market in Warsaw in the late 1990s. Firms reported that they made project location decisions based on whether a particular *gmina* had a pro-development attitude and expeditious handling of applications.

The period that is most informative for this study is the second half of the 1990s, when the private supply of housing increased substantially. During this time, a good working relationship with the local *gmina* proved crucial in the development approval process. It was the local authority who could make or break a project by expediting bureaucratic processing. Once the *gmina* supported a project, it would also help protect the project from contests from other interest groups during the approval process. So it is not surprising that a firm's decisions on project location were influenced by both the market and the *gminas'* orientation and efficacy. The property rights risks were reduced through the help of individual local bureaucrats.

Similar to HCMC, starting in December 2003 development authority was recentralized to Warsaw city. Some autonomous *gminas* had been diverting public finances earmarked for direct public services to other projects, such as new council offices, and some had allowed development even where it violated the city's master plan. Such practices made it difficult to coordinate larger-scale transportation and infrastructure projects. But when development authority was recentralized, development projects ground to a halt because the shift complicated the presale contracting method of investment financing and discouraged landowners from selling property dependent on approval and permitting by the city.

Despite the many similarities between the two markets, some important differences emerged in the way Warsaw's market functioned, and these differences are related to Warsaw's more conventional set of transition reforms. The property cadastre institution, which records ownership, has made a significant impact on both project financing and market expansion through the growth of the mortgage industry. Table 6.5 shows the rapid growth in banks' residential mortgage portfolios since the mid-1990s. The banks require registered title in order to make loans, and the bank mortgages are in turn efficiently registered in district courts. The majority of the customers of the firms interviewed in this study used bank mortgages to buy their future units. In fact, the sales offices of the more successful developers provide information about mortgage financing products along with information on the housing units they are selling.

But as in HCMC, the consumers bear the major risks. Borrowers obtain mortgages for unbuilt units that the developers have presold to them in order to finance the housing project. Yet borrowers can obtain title only for a completed unit, which on average takes about two years to build. If for some reason

Table 6.5   The Polish residential mortgage portfolio, 1995–2001

Year	Annual increase (PLN millions)	Annual change (percentage)	Cumulative portfolio (PLN millions)
1995	244.4	—	244.4
1996	492.4	101	736.8
1997	777.6	58	1514.4
1998	1395.1	79	2909.5
1999	2104.8	51	5013.8
2000	4500.0	114	9513.8
2001	4600.0	48	13800.0

Source: Dr. Jacek Laszek, NBP in REAS Konsulting. 2002. *Warsaw residential market report 2002/2003*. Warsaw: REAS.

the development company does not deliver the unit, the buyer still owes the mortgage but cannot deliver the collateral, and the banks can then go after the borrower's personal assets. The buyer could hypothetically take the firm to court, but his or her position is often weak compared to that of the creditors.[7]

Reusable Norms about Legality

Poland's transition is considered successful because its transition policies emphasized strengthening legal private property rights to promote investment. And in all interviews, firms clearly put a great emphasis on creating documents that conveyed the legal nature of transactions. For example, they repeatedly mentioned notarization of documents as an important part of all real estate transactions.[8] "This is a country obsessed with stamps—it's traditional" explained a Polish expatriate real estate consultant who had returned to Poland from the United Kingdom in 1991. Yet while documents may be notarized, an Office of Consumer Protection survey of contracts made by housing developers found that many contracts do not have the necessary legal form (Lopinski 2005).

The norms concerning legality are not especially surprising in light of Poland's long history of private property rights in the Civil Code tradition, rooted in Roman law and the Napoleonic Code. The modern institution of mortgaging property was actually invented in the nineteenth century in Silesia, which is now in Poland. Since 1918, Poland has had a system of title registration called "mortgage books" that integrates three historical systems—Russian, German, and Austrian. At that time, banks started to use properties as loan collateral and mortgage bonds as a means of securitizing bank portfolios. These private property institutions were not completely eradicated during the Communist regime in Poland. Even though after World War II many properties were nationalized and communalized, the majority of small farmers, individual homeowners, and owners of units in multifamily buildings in the periphery retained their titles.[9] Transactions of farmland and houses in the provinces were performed as before, with proper registration in the mortgage books in special courts. With the beginning of political and economic transition in 1989, many elements of the pre-socialist institutions of property rights could be resumed.

Poland did not simply revert to its pre-socialist legal institutions, however. Multilateral development organizations, such as U.S. Agency for International Development (USAID) and the World Bank, cofinanced foreign advisers to help draft new laws and ordinances, such as the *Condominium Law* and *Mortgage Fund Regulations*, in order to more effectively connect property to modern capital markets. But this external intervention in the reform of property rights was constrained by the institutional capacity of the Polish judicial system.

> The transformation from communism to democracy, reports the *Financial Times*, did not guarantee that democratic institutions would function properly. "Institutions were imported from the west without making sure they could function.... According to the U.S. Department of State [m]any investors—foreign and domestic—complain

about the slowness of the judicial system...investors often voice concern about frequent or unexpected issuance of or changes in laws and regulations." (Heritage Foundation 2004, 320)

Thus, participants in Warsaw's housing market placed great importance on notaries and contracts even though they were not readily enforceable and were disconnected from the post-Communist versions of property law. Instead, the legal tradition and norms that served the old Polish capitalist system could be reused to fit a constellation of interests that differed from what we saw in HCMC: to solidify the transition from Communism. Local government support of a private housing industry that welcomed foreign investment and property ownership and the development of a private mortgage banking industry were supported by the newly democratic Poland, which pursued an overarching goal to join the European Union. The industry also had popular support from Poles who were reembracing capitalism and seeking privately owned apartments.

The alignment of these interests supported the rise of private land development firms. Still, there were practical and financial gaps in developing projects. The entrepreneurs bridged these gaps, using the ambiguity in "legal," notarized contracts, which carried social legitimacy, to renegotiate prices with land sellers and customers who had few feasible alternatives.

Not Learning from One Another:
Attention and Social Structure

Saying the past matters does not necessarily mean that countries must have a history of capitalism in order to have capitalism. Even if one's grandfather might have lived in pre-Communist Poland, how does that ancestry practically help one determine how to develop real estate in Warsaw today? The Warsovians also needed to learn capitalism, a new post-socialist capitalism. Research into the emergence of entrepreneurs in the industrial sectors in other Central European countries has also found that social cognitive processes better explain the process of institutional change. Eyal, Szelenyi, and Townsley conclude that in the Czech Republic and Hungary, neither property ownership, political capital, nor social networks explain who become entrepreneurs. Rather, the phenomenon required people to collectively reinterpret their roles and draw on shared experiences, ways of knowing, and common understandings (Eyal, Szelenyi, and Townsley 1998).

But as they translated those interests into actions, the Warsaw developers differed from their HCMC counterparts in how they learned capitalism. While entrepreneurs in HCMC reported that they needed networks with one another in order to "survive," the Polish interviewees unanimously agreed that there was little social networking among real estate developers in Warsaw. Apparently, they neither contact one another for formal business purposes nor socialize informally. The fierce competition for good sites and customers offers the main reason for this difference. No one could recall an example of cooperating for mutual gain. An expatriate real estate consultant who has been working in Poland since 1991 argued that Poland's business culture differs from those in the United States, the United Kingdom, and Germany where he had worked previously. In these countries even competing parties can see that a deal can potentially offer gains to both sides while Poles tend to think in stark terms of winners and losers. "They are happy to start negotiating but it is hard to come to a decision because there is a sense that you might be one-upped." He attributes this lack of trust to the environment fostered during the socialist regime. The lack of social networking and trust among the development firms does not encourage the use of alternatives to legal business relations.[10]

Instead, Polish entrepreneurs seem to have learned most from foreigners. Several key informants report that the formation of Warsaw's firms developed in stages. During the early 1990s, real estate developers in Poland were primarily foreigners providing housing for their corporate clients. These foreign firms hired local staff who could better navigate the Polish bureaucracy. They trained these staff in business classes and on the job. As transition progressed, the local staffs branched out and started their own firms. Later on, returning Polish expatriates who had gained experience overseas in real estate in Europe and the United States founded new domestic firms.

Some of the theorists who have examined the role of culture in promoting entrepreneurialism claim that individualistic cultures were a key factor of capitalism in the West (Greif 2006), while others point to the collective, networked cultures in the miraculously rapid rise of capitalism in the East. Given the variation in empirical outcomes, these factors must be dependent on other intervening factors.

The comparisons made here lead us to the issues of where a particular society's attention lies and intersubjectivity. Conventional policymakers attribute Central Europe's success in transitioning to a market economy to having the right policies in a universal sense. But this chapter suggests that the reforms were appropriate because Poles were attentive to western European institutions. It fit with the way Polish society valued the same objects that the policies were pushing: titled property rights, mortgage markets, and foreign investment.

Chinese Fiscal Socialism

Of all the urban transition cases, China has probably received the most scholarly attention. China represents another example of a country that did not pursue the conventional transition economic reforms but has grown tremendously. Real estate is one of its explosively growing economic sectors, and private firms have grown rapidly, producing the majority of new housing developments. Scholars who have examined the way China's private housing markets function note many of the same dynamics we observed in HCMC. With the onset of transition, China saw a major demographic movement toward urbanization as migrants poured into major cities. Similarly, the state owns all land but allows private, transferable land use rights. China pursued a development strategy different from the earlier generation of Asian miracle economies by decentralizing many aspects of its authority to local government, leading to diversity and experimentation in economic development strategies. People sometimes call this decentralization a necessity because of China's large size, but we saw the same dynamic in Vietnam, which is much smaller.

In any case, Chinese cities also have the fiscal socialism system that I described in HCMC in chapter 4. In large cities such as Beijing, city district governments also looked for extrabudgetary sources of financing and leveraged their control of land management. China scholars in urban planning and political economy focus primarily on the relationship between two groups within the system: private firms and local government. In particular, scholars view the local government as being as entrepreneurial as the firms (Oi 1995; Duckett 1998; Wu 2002; Zhu 2004). Others have looked at the alliances that have been formed between the local government and the emerging elite into growth coalitions (Zhu 1999). Urban scholars have argued that this dynamic is not unique to developing countries but is a global trend, as public finances increasingly come from private corporations who look to the government to decrease their investment risks (Harvey 1989).

This literature, however, does not conceive of the transition as a wider societal project, reflecting scholarship's division between those who study urban issues and those who study rural areas—when what we are observing is their interaction on the urban periphery. The activist and Chinese social movement literatures do focus on the other groups in society that have been negatively affected by fiscal socialism, namely the unemployed and displaced. The literature on rural Chinese resistance indicates that one strategy has been to increase the divide between central and local government, just as we saw in Vietnam. By framing their demand for more compensation as one that more fully complies with central government policy or laws, resisters appeal to the central government to use their authority to override local abuses (Li and O'Brien 1996). They claim they are not agitating to create social change but rather to receive their rightful share.

The proliferation of protests around land issues has increased dramatically in number and violence over the last 10 years (Tanner 2005). Interestingly, some critics of China's fiscal socialism have framed Vietnam's transition as the more progressive and democratic. For example, Chinese newspaper reports focus on Vietnam's political institutions, which are said to be more accountable to citizens than China's. Some also marvel at how Vietnam's land and real estate markets seem to represent a genuinely open market in comparison to China's. This backhanded way of criticizing the Chinese government by praising a smaller, lower-income country has not gone unnoticed, as the Chinese Communist Party has now banned public discussion of Vietnam's transition (Abrami, Malesky, and Zheng 2007). Another distinction between the Chinese and Vietnamese housing industries is that the structure of China's market is dominated by very large firms, with few small and medium enterprises, making it more difficult for new firms to enter this market. Chinese city and district governments have also encouraged investment by foreigners who continued to invest heavily during the Asian currency crisis (Hsing 1998).

There is much more research on China than can be discussed in this book. Here, the point is to indicate the major similarities and differences between Chinese and Vietnamese transition to a private land development industry.

Essentials of the Transition and Varieties of Capitalism

Some might think that the variation between Vietnam and China, let alone between the Asian and European transitions, is not especially important. Burawoy argues that studying variations in capitalism masks the bottom line of bureaucracy domination, which coordinates interests operating at all levels of society. Other sociologists, however, take issue with the neo-Marxist agenda of discussing capitalism's internal contradiction at the expense of any other research agendas. They argue that the dichotomy between elites and workers is less relevant in the recent transitions (Eyal, Szelenyi, and Townsley 2001; Stark and Bruszt 2001). While classical sociologists saw capitalism as a unitary system, neoclassical sociology accounts for the empirical differences by examining the process and agents of social change (Swedberg 2005).

In comparing the four transition cases, we found that the variations in capitalist institutions do have important material and political implications. The case outcomes varied in terms of political participation, wealth distribution, and more specifically, the government's influence in negotiating the land transfer terms from the rural population. Private firms were not able to form in Hanoi. China has experienced growing violence over land conversions. Warsaw had significantly less acrimony over land use conversions on the city's periphery.[11] They were helped by the fact that most rural landholders retained their private property rights even during the Communist era, and thus they were in a position of selling their land to the developers rather than seeking compensation for relocation. In contrast to Vietnam, Warsovians unhappy with the private developers' projects had an institutionalized means of raising their objections during the development approval process, which required community input. Furthermore, the solidarity movement in Poland's transition made the population especially supportive of the new managerial elite in power and their strategies to transition to a market economy (Eyal, Szelenyi, and Townsley 1998).

While the comparison of the transition cases presented in this chapter acknowledges their very different social contexts, the examination does confirm Burawoy's assessment of the essentials of transition. In each case the key reason for a firm's successful emergence was the devolution of planning authority to the sub-city level of government, the city districts. These units started negotiating with emerging private land developers to exchange land development rights for infrastructure development. This decentralized negotiation of land transfers could not be conducted at the national level because it involves an exchange that weakens the government's legitimizing claim of serving the general public's interest. It was especially problematic in the Asian transition countries, where the state retained ownership of land, one of the pillars of the Communist revolution. But it is important to note that this arrangement could not have happened without the large numbers of households who willingly bought into the new housing industry despite the many risks involved. The terms of the arrangements were also contested in all cases, however, and in both Warsaw and HCMC the private negotiations between city districts and private firms were so socially problematic that planning authority was eventually recentralized.

Furthermore, in order for this socially difficult transfer of land control to occur, a corresponding change in social cognition needed to develop in order to enable it. An entrepreneur could not decide to start developing a project without a corresponding change in roles, relationships, and ultimately new actions and dispositions in the rest of society. I diagrammed this paradigm shift in figure 4.1. Because the social cognition process of change was not engaged in Hanoi, prospective entrepreneurs eventually moved south.

My comparative analysis further articulates that *how* this change in social cognition happened in the transition cases varied according to the cultural schema available to a given society. Culture entails cognitive resources that can be reconceptualized and deployed in making the transition comprehensible. Thus the new paradigm spread in different ways in each case, according to the pathways of its social structures. The transition in HCMC was assisted by the extensiveness and openness of its social networks in rapidly disseminating new ideas and by its social norms, which allowed a laxness in following regulations—even by local bureaucrats—and experimentation in private contracting. The changes in social cognition facilitated the realignment of interests to support the problematic transfer of land and the large numbers of entrepreneurial private firms entering the market. In Warsaw, the transfer was assisted by developers taking advantage of the legitimacy of legal paraphernalia and Poland's desire to join the western European economy; the spread of information and paradigms occurred less through social networking and more through vicarious learning from foreigners.

Notes

1. Other studies have also found that industrial firms and their suppliers in Vietnam use informal contracting (Woodruff and McMillan 1999).

2. Apparently this is not an anomaly; Hanoi had distributed only 11% of certificates by 1999.

3. For more detailed and technical discussion of the specification of the models used in this study, see Kim (2004).

4. A multiyear data set would have been desirable, but previous years' issues were unavailable because the archives for the Hanoi edition were destroyed in a flood.

5. For a more rigorous analysis of why alternative hypotheses and endogeneity issues did not compromise these findings, see the discussion in the original articles (Kim 2004, 2007)

6. The Heritage Foundation also praised Poland's economy as "one of the most successful and open in Central Europe" and ranked it 31 out 155 countries around the world in terms of its promotion of free markets (Heritage Foundation 2004).

7. Two institutions were emerging to deal with this risk: gap insurance during the construction period and escrow accounts to protect the funds.

8. Every *voivodship* (province) in Poland has its own association of legal counselors and notaries. Private notaries play a particularly important role in checking whether the contract is legal and in bearing witness to it. In order to become a notary, one must obtain a master of law degree and pass a credentialing exam. The notaries were an institutionalized part of public administration before and during the Communist years. In the early 1990s notaries became private entities, but their fees are regulated by the government.

9. Properties owned or abandoned by Nazis were nationalized after the Communist takeover, but the old property registers were not destroyed, fueling restitution disputes especially in the city center, where the redevelopment value of land is higher.

10. The Polish Homebuilders Association is an organization whose mission is to enable social networking between firms, influence public policies, and provide information and education to its members. It has 700–1,000 members (individuals and firms), with about 150 in Warsaw. But my case firms, one of which was led by the former head of the association, still confirm the lack of practical networking between firms.

11. See note 9 for how this was different in the city center.

7

Conclusion

This book has considered a puzzle: why have some countries transitioned to capitalism so rapidly? How did they change their economies so fundamentally when so many reform efforts in developing countries have been ineffective? The conundrum has grown the last two decades as transition countries in Europe and Asia attempted to overhaul their entire economic systems with varying results. We must concede that a particular set of reforms does not correlate with economic growth, investment, and domestic firm formation. Vietnam is one of the most curious cases of transition, because while experts have ranked it as having the most inappropriate reforms, it is currently one of the fastest growing economies in the world.

I have focused on solving one part of Vietnam's transition puzzle. Its fastest growing city, Ho Chi Minh City, has a real estate industry that ranks as the worst place in the world for private capital to invest.[1] Nevertheless, Vietnam's domestic housing market has flourished. And most intriguingly, hundreds of entrepreneurs and private firms emerged within the first decade of transition to develop large investment projects. Where did these people come from? How could they conduct business in such an inhospitable economic environment? The aim of my research was to help fill the gap in our understanding of economic transition by directly engaging this first generation of entrepreneurs. I lived in Vietnam and developed extended case studies to find answers. Collecting original data was necessary, because while there is a voluminous amount of scholarship on capitalism and Communism, the puzzles of the recent transitions require us to go back to the ground and look afresh at what is happening in order to revise our theories so that they connect better with the empirical evidence.

Solving the mystery of Vietnamese capitalism required me to let go of the assumption that real estate development followed the same steps found in developed, western markets. I first had to find what these developers were actually doing—all the actions they took to form and develop housing projects. This led to identifying a development process that defied conventional wisdom. For example, the entrepreneurs started investing in a project before receiving official investment approval to use the site. In order to understand why this particular development paradigm emerged, I explored why they chose these particular actions from the range of possible actions. Finding the boundaries on the set of actions that were considered and not considered helped to locate the structural constraints in this transition economy. Within these constraints, I found that the firms found many ways to develop projects in HCMC. But, as other institutionalist scholars in many disciplines started to recognize at the turn of the century, we need to ask a more fundamental question: How did they know what to do and how to do it? How did they change from what they were doing before Vietnam's transition to their new identities and actions? What are the processes of institutional change?

My research eventually led me to the concept of social cognition. Social cognition's framework provides insights into the process of institutional change that better explain the diversity of transition outcomes than either the historical materialist or the neoclassical frameworks. It illuminates how market capitalism developed so rapidly in Vietnam despite conventional wisdom, why political connections and financial resources were not enough to determine the success of firms, why private firms did not emerge as readily in Hanoi as they did in HCMC, and why developers in Warsaw, Poland, emerged under the conventional set of reforms. This final chapter elaborates how processes of social cognition account for the various empirical findings of this study.

Learning from the New Capitalists

I realized that my case firms, despite being an eclectic group in terms of size and productivity, ownership, domestic and foreign participation, political power, and social position, all shared a common understanding of the way private land development works in HCMC. This fiscal socialism system, outlined in chapter 4, was not recorded in any government economic development plan or in any urban economics textbook. Still, my fieldwork enabled me to diagram the system, and the entrepreneurs confirmed their roles in it and the terms of their new economic relationships. Their understanding of the terms of fiscal socialism distinguished these entrepreneurs from lay dabblers in real estate (who might, for example, build an extension to their house in order to rent rooms). This motley group of entrepreneurs possessed a new and shared cognitive paradigm.

The fiscal socialism model of land development was not only a significant change for Vietnam, but also completely unlike the conventional model of the way land development is supposed to work in a market economy—the model that development projects, overseas technical assistance, and capacity building projects presuppose. Rather than having secure property rights and enforcement of contracts through courts to encourage private investment, property titles were distributed *after* the land rights were sold, the project was financed by customers, and the construction was completed. Because it seems untenably risky to invest in property one does not own, policy experts have consistently viewed Vietnam's institutional framework as severely backward for a market economy. The obvious question arises as to why the fiscal socialism system emerged, rather than the conventional one. My fieldwork showed that both power and cognition were key.

The state played a large role in the construction of fiscal socialism because it controls all land development through ownership, urban planning, and permits and approvals. Its bureaus decide which land parcels may be developed by private parties and thus which current land occupants must eventually relocate. But HCMC's private market and entrepreneurialism did not form in response to a grand master plan designed by the state. For one thing, the government does not have the public finance to develop most of its plans. Nor can it command private entities to perform, as it could with state-owned enterprises during the era of central planning. Rather, the way the new system was structured requires a definition of power broader than state coercion and the manipulation of political elites.

Some theorists have defined power as the strategic alignment of interests. The state needed public finance to fund the infrastructure development of its rapidly sprawling city and to bolster its legitimacy. Meanwhile, large segments of the exploding urban population, whose household incomes had tripled through trading, were seeking better housing options after decades of public neglect, as well as investment opportunities for their surplus. In the beginning of transition, with the city's need for heavy capital investments for economic development but without effective means for the state to access private savings, the firms filled a role in mediating the interests of these parties. They were the dealmakers who could take household savings and build the city's infrastructure. But the rural population contested the share they received for being dispossessed and relocated for new urban development projects, to the point that they also shaped the terms of the land transfer and the firms' project location, size, and profitability. In other words, the less powerful members of society still had an important role in shaping the social construction of fiscal socialism through their resistance.

Identifying the alignment of interests helps us understand why the various social groups would choose to participate in the new economic system. But for these people to see and adapt to the new order required a socialization process. In other words, the reformation of the economy involved reconstructing cognitive paradigms in society as well as in the developers. One indication of the social cognition process is to observe how power struggles were fought in public discourse. The central and local governments faced limited resistance through public demonstrations and editorials in state-run media, but these acts were just the tip of the iceberg of social dissent that the state could not ignore. Society had generated several narratives about the transition, such as stories about the greediness of ward officials and private developers. But it had also generated narratives about the greediness of farmers and the need for rapid economic development. The tension between these competing narratives did not have a primary forum, such as a supreme court; rather, interpretive narratives and knowledge about conflicts and acts of resistance spread throughout society into its cognitive collective. The new economic system and the very material transfers of land and finance were enabled and shaped by the boundaries and definitions being constructed through this society-wide negotiation process.

Furthermore, the strategic alignment of interests throughout society is still not enough to explain how the firms could turn potential opportunities into reality. By Western standards, the substantial risks in this arrangement should still have inhibited investment. I observed that within the new paradigm of fiscal socialism, the firms that emerged still had to find practical ways to manage the risks and make projects work. Specifically, in order for the case firms to complete the four critical steps in urban land development projects, they had to create institutional arrangements of their own through private contracting and relationships. In chapter 3 I outlined the considerable institutional diversity in the ways the firms found land to develop, negotiated land compensation, collected development finance, and processed the many permits and approvals needed. The creation of these practical micro-institutional arrangements allowed HCMC's unusual market to function with formal project approval and property titles distributed at the end of the project, customers supplying the bulk of development capital, and local government working closely with the developers.

As expected, I found that the firms' ability to create these institutions were in part constrained by their social position. The entrepreneurs were relatively young, educated urbanites. However, fieldwork in HCMC also showed that in the unruly social construction process, developers who were in similar social positions, and who had similar access to political resources, did not interact with the changing structures in the same way. In order to survive, all firms had to learn how to develop projects. They did not necessarily copy what other firms or actors did, but they did acquire tacit knowledge vicariously. In other words, agents started to perceive the underlying framework of new possible economic actions and sometimes generated behavior going beyond what they had seen or heard. The developers exhibited agency in the particular choices they made about how to develop projects that were important in determining such things as which firms succeeded in HCMC. The most productive firms, although varying in size and ownership, shared a common factor: their leadership continually learned and adopted new information and strategies into their operations. They learned how to be entrepreneurs in this particular market.

Thus the reformation of the entrepreneurs' cognitive paradigms made fiscal socialism practicable. Social cognition, however, means that the cognitive paradigms change not in just individuals but in the other members of society with whom they interact. Very important in understanding the change in these entrepreneurs is the change in some bureaucrats, in particular local wards and districts, that made fiscal socialism a practical reality in HCMC. Their discretion in interpreting and implementing the national laws and policies and becoming entrepreneurial themselves in trying new activities and relationships were key to the successful completion of projects. That is, it was not only the firms that learned, but also the local state actors who learned how to be a capitalist-friendly state. This was not true of all bureaucrats that I met, some of whom still spoke of the immorality of the private sector's existence. But my case firms freely introduced me to local bureaucrats who thought differently and with whom they could work.

Furthermore, the vicarious learning exhibited by the developers and local state actors was assisted by HCMC's informal social structures more than the formal, legal ones. The spread of entrepreneurialism in HCMC was shaped by the openness and extensiveness of its social networks and the availability of intermediaries. People were open to meeting people and sharing information. New people could enter the market without extremely strong political connections because they could develop them. Furthermore, the looser social norms about laws and regulations held by the bureaucracy in the south encouraged people to experiment and create new economic relations.

The importance of these informal, social structures and their cognitive nature became even clearer when we compared HCMC's situation to that of Hanoi. Although both cities are in the same country, with uniform laws and policies, and both have very high housing demand, private development firms did not emerge in Hanoi as they did in HCMC. Local political economy interests and social norms embedded in both state and private actors impacted the formation of markets. Several of the firms that had successful operations in HCMC tried to develop projects in Hanoi, in order to take advantage of the severe housing shortage there. But they reported that the closed power structure in Hanoi limited entry into the market, as did the more exacting regulatory enforcement by local bureaucrats. It was more than the bureaucracies that impeded the formation of firms, however. As evidenced in the statistical analysis of market prices in both cities, presented in chapter 6, households in Hanoi's new housing market possessed such deeply embedded norms about legal formalism that they would reduce the asking price of their own properties if they did not have property title papers in hand. In short, the fiscal socialism system could not have emerged in Hanoi because neither the political economy nor the cognitive structures allowed sufficient agency in state and private actors to create new relations and actions. That is, even if individual agents had had simple profit maximizing interests (instead of the social, interdependent ones we observed), they would have had difficulty performing entrepreneurial actions because the rest of society was not willing to engage with them. Which district officials would protect their projects? How many Hanoian households would pay installments for an unbuilt house for which they would not receive title until several years later? Individual Hanoians who wanted to enter the real estate business could relocate to the south and work there, but the reverse was not true. The unimaginability of new relations and actions is central to the variation we observe in transition economies.

This comparative example does not imply that Hanoi does not have the right cultural traits for capitalism, or that HCMC was somehow more naturally entrepreneurial. For example, around 2003, after the central government changed the top leadership in HCMC (something it does on a regular basis), the newly installed bureaucrats enforced a more formal and exact reading of the regulations and closer oversight of district government activity. Concurrently, popular criticism increasingly vilified the land management practices of some local ward and district officials. The other HCMC state actors then became less amenable to suppressing the bargaining ability of rural landholders and facilitating the firms' applications for development approval through the many intergovernmental layers. HCMC's fiscal socialism system of land development slowed to a crawl, if not a halt. Because of a change in powerful agents and narratives about bureaucrats, the paradigm shifted so that the local state actors changed their dispositions. It also improved the farmers' bargaining position in relocation compensation. The market and its terms of exchange are being continuously reconstructed by agents in society.

In other words, the rate of entrepreneurialism between the two cities varied because cognitive changes are not independent of society. While national legal and policy reforms could matter insofar as the degree of agency they allow, how much is taken depends on local social norms and power alliances that can vary even within the same country. We saw that in contrast to Hanoi, HCMC's relatively looser social norms about property rights and legality meant that some agents in the local district and ward bureaus exercised discretion when planning authority was decentralized to them and some agents in the private sphere experimented with new economic relations and transactions. The open social networks shaped a process of transition that involved people in HCMC watching and learning from one another.

However, the kinds of social networking and social norms present in HCMC were not necessary for private investment in other places. Another important insight of social cognition theory is that attention is not located in the same places in particular societies. In a comparative analysis with Warsaw, we saw that Polish developers did not learn how to develop projects from one another and did not collaborate or socialize with one another. Instead of networking, they paid attention to foreign firms and learned from them as unofficial apprentices. We also saw that Warsovians were sticklers about legal documents and notaries, much like Hanoians. But the firms took advantage of legal formalism and redeployed it in the post-Communist housing system. Despite being touted as an exemplar of conventional transition reforms, most of Warsaw's property contracts were not formally correct nor could they readily be enforced in courts. Their social legitimacy, however, could still be used to encourage customers to take risky full-recourse mortgages to pay for unbuilt properties and for landholders to sell development options to the new firms. As in HCMC, the key to firms being able to implement projects was the decentralization of development authority to the sub-city, *gmina* level of government. Some *gminas* would exercise discretion and help the firms gain planning approval to proceed with a project. In other words, Warsaw's housing market bore striking resemblances to HCMC's fiscal socialism.

In summary, housing markets and private firms developed rapidly in HCMC and Warsaw through a reconstruction of socially shared cognition that supported a strategic re-alignment

of interests. This new paradigm, along with practical knowledge, spread through social processes of vicarious learning and
the particular pathways of attention structured by their respec-
tive societies. The location of these happened to be in very different places between the transition societies. Entrepreneurs in
Vietnam did not pay much attention to foreigners, but rather
paid a great deal of attention to one another and local authorities. Meanwhile, as Poland headed toward joining the European
Union, its entrepreneurs paid a great deal of attention to foreigners, particularly those from western Europe, who were actively
buying property and making investments from the beginning
of transition.

The Nature of Capitalism

The discussion up until now has focused on the question of how
entrepreneurs emerged in transition countries. But if we take a
moment to observe what has happened, we find a process very
different from the policy literature's descriptions of the transition to capitalism. Even though I just emphasized how differently societies can reconstruct their economies depending on
both structures and individual agents, the comparison between
HCMC, Warsaw, and major Chinese cities also revealed some
important similarities between their transitions. On the sur-
face, they have been viewed as having taken completely diver-
gent reform paths, with Poland being identified as an exemplar
because of its law-based economic liberalization reforms that
welcomed foreign capital and Vietnam and China categorized
as outlier cases. Yet when we observe the entrepreneurs and
how they developed investment projects, rather than focusing
on policies, we find that developers in all three rapid transition
cases acted in a surprisingly similar fashion. Key to the takeoff of private investment in these cities was the decentralization of land use planning and permitting authority to a sub-city
level bureau, the districts and the *gminas*, which encouraged

discretionary acts. The successful firms were those who could do three things. First, they could locate individuals within the local bureaucracy who would protect their project through the many hurdles needed to gain and maintain land control. Second, they could take advantage of the local social norms and cultural resources to generate a steady stream of development capital from members of the public who took on the considerable risk of buying into projects before they were built. Third, they were enabled to remove the people currently occupying the land parcels by the new narratives constructed in society and active local government support.

These three key elements are present, irrespective of the official reform paths taken. Furthermore, social conflict around these issues abounds in the transition economies. Both Vietnamese and Polish developers identified site control as by far the most difficult hurdle for them. In both HCMC and Warsaw, as public sentiment grew against the private deals entrepreneurs were negotiating with local government, planning authority was eventually recentralized in the name of protecting the public interest. This classic planning issue of the balance between the roles of the state and market in society is continuously renegotiated in higher-income countries as well (Harvey 1989).

The crux of this conflict in transitioning to a private real estate industry involves the transfer of property rights to private developers. A change in social cognition must occur in order for this transfer of property to happen. Urban development could not take place unless different members of society were able to move into new reciprocal roles and negotiate the terms of this transfer. The outcome of this change in social cognition, however, varied between the transition cases in terms of the openness and equity of the transfer of property. While the uninformed might have undersold the value of their property in the early days of Poland's transition, the state did not routinely pressure them to undersell. Another major difference from the Asian transition cases is that landholders on Warsaw's periphery started transition with stronger property rights, as they had retained ownership under the Communist government, and private ownership gained even greater social standing during the post-Communist period. Moreover, community and environmental interest groups' concerns were included in the formal investment approval process and thus could delay projects. To address the occasional undermining of the social trust needed for households to buy into projects early, Poland developed more regulations and insurance institutions. Meanwhile, in both Vietnam and China, the lack of openness and equity in the land transfer process led to widespread social conflict and protest. Developers were imprisoned and given harsh sentences. In Vietnam, as in Poland, land use planning authority was eventually recentralized from the district to the city level as a result of the public outcry leaving developers to negotiate compensation directly with farmers, which changed the terms of the land transfer. This development has not yet occurred in practice in China.

Transition policy advice, however, does not address this fundamental transfer of property that has to take place in a capitalist system. Rather, the transition policy literature treats "privatization" as almost a technical or a state-centered activity, listing percentages and rates of state asset sales. The policy literature often seems exasperated by the slow rates of privatization, which it assumes are primarily the result of elites hoarding assets. We should be more forthright in acknowledging that the transition to capitalism at the end of the twentieth century involved decentralized, local negotiations of transferring property to private hands in exchange for development. This is *the* major social reconstruction project in transition, and, not surprisingly, it is contested both materially and cognitively.

Cognitive Processes and Implications for International Development

People can change and society can change, as they did in these transition countries. The question I have dealt with concerns how change happens, the process of institutional change. If the institutions that matter are those that are practiced, how then do practices change? The predominant approaches to understanding institutional change hold that people change their actions when it is in their best interest to do so, while other theories dwell on how we have been influenced to change by either strategic or evolutionary processes. But this study questions the value of the search for one universal driver of human behavioral change. In the variety of transition outcomes, some factors, such as the rule of law or levels of foreign investment, seem to be more important in one case and less important in another. By bringing institutional change under the rubric of social construction processes, which incorporate social cognition and dispersed and discursive concepts of power, we can better understand why some policies have more impact than others.

Such an understanding has profound implications for current international development policy practice. Mainstream development discourse has persisted with a framework predicated on institutional universals, despite the empirical outcomes that clearly deny this possibility. It is clearly insufficient to assume that the introduction of laws or policies are sufficient to reform an economy, bringing about new economic behaviors and relations throughout society; indeed, such approaches are doomed to failure. A different approach is necessary.

The new social cognition framework starts with the only clear universals available—the mechanisms of human cognitive function. How do people fundamentally change? They have to learn. The new social cognition framework taps into cognitive science research, which can provide insights into the mechanisms behind social change. For one thing, it suggests that we must not only perceive new information but also pay attention to it in order for us to begin changing patterns of thinking and acting. This insight alone has radical implications for international development. Most development policies and projects assume attention for the information and institutional paraphernalia that the project is introducing, and also assume that they will mean the same thing in all societies.

Ironically, however, research into the universals only point more emphatically to the importance of local social structures in defining the currency of attention. Cross-cultural cognitive development literature, as well as long-standing anthropological research, has shown that what people notice as attention-worthy is shaped by a particular society's terms. A good example to counter institutional universalism is the currently popular strategy of distributing property ownership titles for houses and land. We saw that in HCMC new title documents were not the only socially legitimate documents with which to claim and enforce ownership rights. Furthermore, in the market that emerged in HCMC, titles were not used as originally imagined but were withheld until the end of a project in order to leverage all members into playing their roles in the fiscal socialism process of urban land development. Thus new title documents meant something different in HCMC society.

And they also meant something different in Warsaw. People were very attentive to title deed documents and relied on them to participate and invest in the new housing market. Property titles functioned in the market, however, not because of the police power the state could use to enforce legal property rights through courts. Instead, titles, notaries, and other legal vestiges of Poland's long tradition of mortgage documentation were valued signs of legitimacy, not only because private ownership was largely retained during the Communist era in the urban periphery of Warsaw, but also because private ownership was laden with nationalist, anti-Communist symbolism that further legitimized them during the transition period.

The cognitive development literature also suggests that watching others is one of the most powerful ways we acquire and adopt new information and practices. Tacit knowledge and vicarious learning were key to understanding how entrepreneurs became entrepreneurs in both HCMC and Warsaw. In looking at the details of each case, it becomes clear that the changes in their behaviors were not natural but socialized. In HCMC, the firms watched one another, experimented, and found significant help through local state actors and other private agents, and negotiated their new roles. The changes in their actions involved major changes in other actors. The successful foreign businesses in Vietnam did more learning than teaching. Furthermore, the comparative cases showed that the pathways of learning again depended on social structure. In Warsaw, the models were foreigners and returning expatriates with Western experience in real estate, which fit well with Poland's popular goal of joining the European Union and its embrace of foreign investment and ownership.

Again, the implications of vicarious learning for international development practices are profound. In the current trend toward "institution building" and "capacity building" development projects, the focus has been on the training of civil servants through lectures by foreign experts. It is ironic to note that in promoting markets, most of the development work focuses on training bureaucrats who might not be the most influential agents in a society. In any case, this approach has many problematic aspects in practice. The effectiveness of disseminating information through lectures in a classroom setting will differ in appropriateness from society to society, and it may be too far removed from practice to generate any kind of praxis. Furthermore, the impact of the foreign consultants in that process will vary not only by their familiarity with the context and their ability to adapt their material, but also by the kind of attention they will receive in a particular society.

Social cognition theory suggests an alternative approach to international urban development practice. We cannot start by approaching situations with specific institutional paraphernalia to introduce. The Jones Lang Lasalle report that ranked Vietnam as the worst place to invest in real estate, also notes that global investors might be able to successfully invest in heterodox markets if "specific intelligence can be gathered, and safeguards can be put in place, to mitigate some of the risks. Knowledgeable, trustworthy advisers of local partners are especially important to help cross-border market participants navigate markets with lower transparency" (2006, 6). While most people understand that boilerplate solutions usually do not work, what is less clear is what exactly we need to understand about the local context.

Social cognition theory suggests that a more effective orientation for institutional development projects would begin with a different line of questioning. Who will learn? What will they be able to notice and pay attention to? What are the relationships present in this particular society through which people will learn vicariously? How would the people in our project have the opportunity to observe and interact with one another? The answers to these questions will depend on the social structure of the local context and the potential strategic alignment of interests present in a situation. One cannot assume that the reform or intervention will cause notice and effect, or that the intervention would produce the same result in every society.

Of course, we cannot answer with certainty questions about potential strategic alignments, nor can we know a priori which pathways in the social structure will be most efficient. But there is a better chance of effectively engaging the social reconstruction process if members of the society initiate and meaningfully participate in the design of development projects and reforms. This reasoning inspired the trend to increase "ownership" by "clients" and increase grassroots and civil society involvement. Still, as in the case of Poland, there might be cases in which foreign involvement may be a welcomed participant of social reconstruction; it would depend on the relationship of the foreigners to the society.

In either case, development projects should be conceived as potential catalysts of social cognition reconstruction. Most development projects do not have sufficient funds to reform entire systems. Instead, development projects should be seen as a series of interventions used as potential influencers, or to start a series of chain reactions.

This book offers an alternative framework for understanding economic development. It is not meant to replace the contributions previous theories have made about important causal factors in development outcomes, such as legal institutions, the state, networks, culture, and history. Rather, it is a way to integrate and situate them into the processes of institutional change. If we do not address issues of attention and vicarious learning, development projects are likely to continue to be as limited and ineffectual as such projects too often are. The policy discourse in the international development arena would make a greater impact if we conceived of development as an institutional change process rather than a particular institutional framework to be emulated.

Implications for Research

How did the Vietnamese entrepreneurs become capitalists? This study has found that the transition to capitalism is neither the natural propensity of individuals nor the decision of an all-powerful state. It does not necessarily require a long evolutionary process, but instead is a social construction project. The material I have presented shows that the major, rapid, and discontinuous economic change that occurred in Vietnam was fundamentally enabled by a reconstruction of cognitive paradigms shaped by political and social structures and agent actions. Put more simply, this society learned to be capitalist, on its own terms. What is generalizable is not particular legal institutions or policies, but that the process of major economic change involves social cognitive change. Developers in HCMC formulated new schemas and engaged in new behaviors through a highly social, relational process and through a highly political process, in terms of both the state's power and resistance to it. Furthermore, this paradigm shift enabled the transfer of property needed for capitalist land development.

My findings coincide with the recent convergence in the new institutionalist literature that has been reconsidering a social construction perspective of the economy. Recent pragmatist literature in social theory and cross-cultural economic anthropology has also been emphasizing that rather than starting with a preexisting behavioral model of interest, we must recognize that people's behavioral models depend on context and cannot be independent of the situation (Whitford 2002). Grounded, empirical studies of industries have shown that actors in society can create and learn new models (Sabel 1994).

This book incorporates Vygotzky's and Bandura's perspectives on social cognition and discursive notions of power into the social construction framework. Rather than continuing the age-old debate about whether structure or agency trumps the other, the key point is to better understand their interrelationship. The findings presented here show the intimate interdependency between structure and agency. The developer's cognitions were socially shaped into the new paradigm of fiscal socialism. They, and others, reified it by acting out their new roles. This process involved learning, as well as some agency in how developers worked within the structures. Agents could also influence the shaping and reconstruction of structures and material outcomes. But as we saw in the case of Hanoi, agents could not exercise their agency unless others in society were willing to join them. The intriguing duality of structure and agency is that agency requires social cooperation.

Accordingly, while my unit of analysis was the action of entrepreneurs, my findings were not individualistic. Entrepreneurs are often thought of as rugged individualists with good ideas who work hard to bring them to fruition. International development theory is based on the idea that entrepreneurialism is natural and universal, except where it has been grossly inhibited by social and political institutions. When we examine the entrepreneurs in Vietnam, we find not just persons but a society. Entrepreneurialism did not emerge from individuals but from new social relations. The firms could not come into being without corresponding changes on the part of local state actors and consumers in society. Ultimately, entrepreneurs are a social construction.

I hope readers do not miss the irony implicit in the title of this book, which might seem to suggest the exact opposite of its message. So I state explicitly here that the entrepreneurs in Vietnam did not learn capitalism from any foreign experts. They did not learn from a teacher, and they did not learn "the" truth about markets. They created and learned their own reality about their market. I chose the word "learning" to emphasize that capitalism is not a natural state of affairs but rather that the entrepreneurs, as well as local bureaucrats, consumers, and landholders, changed the way they think in order to materially change their world. The changes in social cognition are core to an understanding of Vietnam's transition.

Note

1. See the introducton for further discussion about why this sector is an appropriate one with which to discuss the transition to capitalism more generally.

Appendix
Method of Study

Identification of the Field of Study

The case firms chosen for this study are private land development organizations that, in the period from 1995 to 2001, actively developed infrastructure and residential projects larger than one hectare on the periphery of HCMC, for sale to the general public.

I chose to study this subgroup of new Vietnamese entrepreneurs for many reasons. First, within Vietnam, I focused on Ho Chi Minh City's real estate market because of the magnitude of the physical and institutional changes and its relatively more open and feasible research environment. I decided to focus on those working on projects in the urban periphery of HCMC, because this was the site of some of the largest projects and most rapid development. I limited my cases to firms that were doing larger-scale residential projects, defined as those involving more than one hectare of land. Larger projects are more challenging; they require more capital and coordination as well as the assembly of parcels from several landowners. They also require central government approval in Vietnam. Because of the added challenges of large-scale projects and because of the institutions that can be developed over a number of projects, these organizations are well suited to a comparative analysis of the ways in which they navigate their economic environment.

My final choice was to focus on private organizations. What constitutes "private" is more nuanced in the context of Vietnam's high level of government intervention than it is in a traditional capitalist state. Nevertheless, it is clear that these organizations have more autonomy in their day-to-day operations than the state-owned enterprises I interviewed. Private firms were at a disadvantage as compared to state-owned enterprises in getting timely approvals and financing, so I was curious to learn how they were able to make such large projects feasible. Moreover, by 2000, when I began my longest period of fieldwork, it had become surprisingly easy to conduct interviews with private organizations: government permissions were not needed to hold meetings, and firm members felt free to speak openly in our discussions.

Selection of Cases

After defining the general criteria for the subgroup of private firms I would study, I wanted to make sure that I chose appropriate cases to represent this subgroup. During eight months of fieldwork, from October 2000 to July 2001, I spent the first two months visiting the sites of the new urban development projects that were reshaping HCMC, making a preliminary selection of firms on which to build cases and verifying their suitability with key informants. My informants estimated that roughly 200 private real estate companies were operating in HCMC, with about 40–50 actively developing projects eight years after the 1993 Land Law was promulgated. Using the technique of snowball interviews and my own social networks, I found that there were four types of private land development organizations operating in HCMC. This was not a preconceived framework, but rather one that I conceptualized only after significant fieldwork. I verified the completeness and validity of this typology with key informants associated with land development: bankers, academics, and my case firms themselves. A version of these general types is also corroborated by other studies of Vietnam (Gainsborough 2003).

As mentioned in chapter 2, the four types of firms include investor groups, professional companies, equitized companies, and foreign joint-ventures. Investor groups can be viewed as a variation of the household developers who band together to achieve economies of scale, benefit from any connections and advantages individual members may have, and purchase large sites they could not afford individually. They are flexible groups that form for a specific project, some of which are very large. All of the members have other occupations, and the business does not have a formal office or name. Professional companies, by contrast, have brick-and-mortar offices, a name, and a full-time staff. Equitized firms are formerly state-owned companies that have now been allowed to become private. They can have more autonomy in the management of their operations and access to private capital. Foreign joint-ventures are initiated by foreign investors, who partner with a Vietnamese company and contribute equity to a new entity that may engage in commercial property development and other investment activity in the country.

I should note that these firms pursue development, not land speculation. They have actually invested capital and are adding value to land in order to sell serviced parcels and houses to households. The organizations are private in the sense that they are not state-owned entities. Many of them in fact are owned and managed by former state employees or current state employees who are engaged in private real estate businesses on the side. Furthermore, in some of the companies, state bodies hold minority shares. All are managed privately, however, and are under the purview of private business and land development laws and regulations.

I ended up developing 14 in-depth case studies of private land development organizations in HCMC that had actively pursued projects between 1995 and 2001 (see table 3.1). I subsequently verified through key informants that these firms represented the range of types of private firms that are currently operating in HCMC. I did not choose the cases randomly, nor are they statistically representative. Rather, I wanted to make sure I included a sampling of the variety of firms currently operating in the market. I chose case firms within each of the four types that varied by size, productivity level, and geographic distribution of their projects within the city. I also included all of the significant organizations whose projects are impacting the direction of urban growth in HCMC—that is, the ones everyone talks about in the industry and newspapers.[1]

Identifying Key Economic Actions

Real estate development in any context is a complex endeavor requiring the juggling of many tasks. At the beginning of my fieldwork, I was open to the possibility that different firms might have different development procedures. But because of the strong state control, I found that they all face the same general process (outlined in table 3.2). One can see that despite HCMC being the most streamlined of all Vietnamese cities in terms of land development processes, it is still complicated.

Through my preparatory fieldwork and my open-ended key informant interviews, it became clear that a few of these steps were more challenging than others, and I learned that there were a variety of ways the firms surmounted these challenges. The four steps in the development process that could make or break project feasibility or determine its profitability were: 1) finding land for potential project sites; 2) negotiating a compensation price with the current users, usually farmers; 3) assembling development capital; and 4) processing the many permits and approvals needed to implement the project.

For each case study, I systematically collected several kinds of information. I located the entrepreneurial decision-makers—the ones who decide in which location and how much land they will try to develop, how many units to subdivide the project into, how they will arrange the financing and infrastructure development, and who will be their target market. These decision-makers were people who had been with the organization for a long time and were involved in its day-to-day operations; some were the founder or leaders of the firm or the heads of departments. I first asked these respondents factual questions about their background, noting social identity groups of which they might be a member: hometown region, fields of expertise, university, army, Communist Party membership, and so forth. These easy, nonthreatening questions allowed respondents to become comfortable with the interview situation, but they also enabled me to contextualize their social identity. One of the things I wanted to learn was where these developers came from. Was there some common social position variable that privileged them to become entrepreneurs?

Next, I would ask respondents more easy, factual questions about the history and structure of their organization. This is how I happened to find the parameters of the differences in firm types. It also showed areas where they might have formalized functions in the development process that would indicate which steps in the process take considerable effort.

I next asked them for information about the projects they produce—their location, size, program, and timing. I then began systematically asking more detailed questions about their development projects. I retraced step by step their development process, their considerations in making decisions about their specific projects, and how they implemented each phase. At this point, the interview could go off in a variety of directions, because I wanted to allow them to tell me the way they saw the development process without my imposing a framework or focus of observation. I wanted to be open to new discoveries and the need to alter my research questions.

At the end of the meetings I would ask them about institutional factors that they had not brought up or had mentioned only briefly, in order to probe whether these were an issue in their perception or not. This approach was used in order to capture anything they may have forgotten without biasing the direction of the interview or suggesting answers.

I then followed up with interviews of the network of people they had worked with to develop their projects—these included landbrokers, design and permitting consultant companies, banks, district and ward officials, and government departments. If possible, I spent time in respondents' informal social gatherings. I also interviewed many key informants to get additional insights on these developers, and I asked the developers about one another in order to get some critical perspective on their responses. In addition to these interviews, I visited developers' offices, if they had any, reviewed their project designs and documents, and walked their project sites.

The units of analysis for a comparison of firms of different types and firms with similar political privilege and social position were the four development steps outlined earlier. I retraced with the developers how they were able to overcome the challenges of making the four actions. I also studied how the firms' choices and strategies affected their ability to consistently pull off projects and the number of units they were able to supply, the location of their projects, and project completion time. Firm productivity provides some indicator of the effectiveness of the strategies the firm chose. Profitability indicators would have been ideal, but I could not be certain of an even comparison among the firms' financial data. But given the great housing demand, the availability of investment opportunities in other sectors, open entry and exit in this market, it was reasonable to assume that all projects completed during this period were net positive. The appreciation of residential land value was rapid throughout this period.

Ultimately, I ended up with a large quantity of interview notes that surveyed the real estate industry in HCMC from a variety of perspectives. Besides the members of the case firms and their associates, I had interviewed ministry officials from the central government in Hanoi, HCMC government officials at the city, district, and ward level, and Vietnamese university professors and academics in both Hanoi and HCMC. I interviewed the dominant state-owned companies, banks, property lawyers, and journalists who cover the real estate market.

Note

1. I began contacting various organizations through referrals from key informants and my own social network. The openness to forming and joining new networks is a distinguishing characteristic of HCMC, and it was a major factor in choosing it as my research site. Even so, I was surprised at the extent to which people were forthcoming in comparison to my first visit in 1996. I had tried a number of approaches previously, but what seemed to be the most important factors were my identity as an academic, being introduced personally, and that fact that I was dealing primarily with the private sector.

References

Abrami, Regina, Edmund Malesky, and Yu Zheng. 2007. Vietnam through Chinese eyes: Comparing vertical and horizontal accountability in single-party regimes. Paper presented at "Why Communism didn't collapse: Exploring regime resilience in China, Vietnam, Laos, North Korea, and Cuba," Dartmouth College.

Amsden, Alice H. 1989. *Asia's Next Giant: South Korea and Late Industrialization*. New York: Oxford University Press.

Amsden, Alice H., and Ajit Singh. 1994. The optimal degree of competition and dynamic efficiency in Japan and Korea. *European Economic Review* 38 (3–4): 941–51.

Bandura, Albert. 1986. *Social Foundations of Thought and Action: A Social Cognitive Theory*. Englewood Cliffs, N.J.: Prentice-Hall.

————. 1989. Human agency in social cognitive theory. *American Psychologist* 44 (9): 1175–84.

————. 1997. *Self-efficacy: The Exercise of Control*. New York: W. H. Freeman.

Berger, Peter L., and Thomas Luckman. 1967. *The Social Construction of Reality*. Garden City, N.J.: Anchor Books.

Bertaud, Alain, and Bertrand Renaud. 1995. *Cities without Land Markets: Location and Land Use in the Socialist City*. Washington, D.C: World Bank.

Bourassa, Steven C., and Yu-Hung Hong. 2003. *Leasing Public Land: Policy debates and international experiences*. Cambridge, Mass.: Lincoln Institute of Land Policy.

Bourdieu, Pierre. 1977. *Outline of a Theory of Practice*. New York: Cambridge University Press.

Bourdieu, Pierre. 2005. *The Social Structure of the Economy.* Malden, Mass.: Polity Press.

Box, G. E. P., and D. R. Cox. 1964. An analysis of transformations. *Journal of the Royal Statistical Society, Series B (Methodological)* 26 (2): 211–52.

Burawoy, Michael. 1998. The Extended Case Method. *Sociological Theory* 16 (1): 4–33.

Buckley, Robert M., and Jerry Kalarickal, eds. 2006. *Thirty Years of World Bank Shelter Lending: What Have We Learned?* Washington, D.C.: World Bank.

———. 2001. Neoclassical sociology: From the end of Communism to the end of classes. *American Journal of Sociology* 106 (4): 1099–120.

Buschman, Timothy J., and Earl K. Miller. 2007. Top-down versus bottom-up control of attention in the prefrontal and posterior parietal cortices. *Science* 315: 1860–62.

CELK Center. 2004. Central European Land Knowledge Center introduction: Current news. *CELK Center Newsletter* 1 (July–August): 1–6.

Chinh, Nguyen Ngoc. 1999. Taxation cart placed well before the horse, protest hard-hit farmers. *Vietnam Investment Review,* November 8.

Coase, Ronald H. 1992. The Institutional Structure of Production. *American Economic Review* 82 (4): 713–19.

Cole, D. H., and P. Z. Grossman. 2002. The meaning of property rights: Law versus economics? *Land Economics* 78 (3): 317–30.

Collet, Francois. 2003. Economic Social Action and Social Network Influences. A discussion around Mark Granovetter sociology of economic life. Paper read at European Sociological Association Conference, September 23–26, 2003, at Murcia, Spain.

Dang, Hung Vo, and Gosta Palmkvist. 2001. Sweden–Vietnam cooperation on land administration reform in Vietnam. Sweden International Development Agency.

Dapice, David, Dinh Cung Nguyen, An Tuan Pham, and Van Bui. 2004. History or policy: Why don't northern provinces grow faster? United Nations Development Program Paper for June 2004 Donor Conference, Harvard University, Cambridge, Mass.

Davis, Diane E. 2004. *Discipline and Development: Middle Classes and Prosperity in East Asia and Latin America.* Cambridge and New York: Cambridge University Press.

de Soto, Hernando. 1989. *The Other Path: The invisible revolution in the third world.* New York: Harper and Row.

———. 2000. *The Mystery of Capital: Why Capitalism Triumphs in the West and Fails Everywhere Else.* New York: Basic Books.

Demsetz, Harold. 1967. Toward a theory of property rights. *American Economic Review* 57 (May): 347–59.

Denzau, Arthur T., and Douglass C. North. 1994. Shared mental models: Ideologies and institutions. *Kyklos* 47 (1): 3–31.

Diamond, Jared. 1999. *Guns, Germs, and Steel: The Fates of Human Societies.* New York: W. W. Norton and Company.

DiMaggio, Paul. 1997. Culture and cognition. *Annual Review of Sociology* 23: 263–87.

DiMaggio, Paul J., and Walter W. Powell. 1983. The Iron Cage Revisited: Institutional Isomorphism and Collective Rationality in Organizational Fields. *American Sociological Review* 48 (2): 147–60.

DOLA. 1998. Modernisation of cadastral mapping and land recording project. Hanoi: Vietnam General Department of Land Administration and Western Australia Department of Land Administration.

Dowall, David E., and Giles Clarke. 1991. *A Framework for Reforming Urban Land Policies in Developing Countries.* Washington, D.C.: World Bank.

Dowall, David E., and John D. Landis. 1982. Land-use controls and housing costs: An examination of San Francisco Bay Area communities. *Real Estate Economics* 10 (1): 67–93.

Dowall, David E., and Michael Leaf. 1991. The price of land for housing in Jakarta. *Urban Studies* 28 (5): 707–22.

Duckett, Jane. 1998. *The Entrepreneurial State in China: Real Estate and Commerce Departments in Reform Era Tianjin.* London: Routledge.

Ellickson, Robert. 1991. *Order without Law: How Neighbors Settle Disputes.* Cambridge, Mass.: Harvard University Press.

———. 1993. Property in land. *Yale Law Journal* 102 (6): 1315–1400.

Evans, Peter. 1995. *Embedded Autonomy: States and Industrial Transformation.* Princeton: Princeton University Press.

Evans, Peter, Theta Skocpol, and Dietrich Rueschemeyer, eds. 1985. *Bringing the State Back In.* New York: Cambridge University Press.

Eyal, Gil, Ivan Szelenyi, and Eleanor Townsley. 1998. *Making Capitalism without Capitalists: The New Ruling Elites in Eastern Europe.* New York: Verso.

———. 2001. The utopia of postsocialist theory and the ironic view of history in neoclassical sociology. *American Journal of Sociology* 106 (4): 1121–28.

Festinger, L. 1957. *A Theory of Cognitive Dissonance.* Evanston, Ill.: Row Peterson.

Fforde, Adam, and Stefan de Vylder. 1996. *From Plan to Market: The Economic Transition in Vietnam.* Boulder, Colo.: Westview Press.

Fforde, Adam, and Hy Van Luong. 1996. Regional development in Vietnam: Local dynamics, market forces and state policies. In *Eastern Asia Policy Papers, 13.* Ontario: University of Toronto and York University.

Forester, John. 1993. *Critical Theory, Public Policy, and Planning Practice: Toward a Critical Pragmatism.* Albany: State University of New York Press.

Foucault, Michel. 1976. *La Volonté de Savoir.* Vol. 1 of *Histoire de la sexualité.* Paris: Gallimard.

Fritsch, Michael. 2004. Entrepreneurship, entry and performance of new business compared in two growth regimes: East and West Germany. *Journal of Evolutionary Economics* 14: 525–42.

Gainsborough, Martin. 2002a. Beneath the veneer of reform: The politics of economic liberalisation in Vietnam. *Communist and Post-Communist Studies* 35: 353–68.

———. 2002b. Understanding Communist transition: Property rights in Ho Chi Minh City in the late 1990s. *Post-Communist Economies* 14 (2): 227–43.

———. 2003. *Changing Political Economy of Vietnam: The Case of Ho Chi Minh City*. New York: Routledge Curzon.

———. 2005. Between exception and rule: Ho Chi Minh City's political economy under reform. *Critical Asian Studies* 37 (3): 363–90.

Garfinkel, Harold. 1967. *Studies in Ethnomethodology*. Englewood Cliffs, N.J.: Prentice-Hall.

Gillespie, John. 1999. Land management for a real estate market. Report, World Bank Urban Upgrading Mission, Ho Chi Minh City.

———. 2001. Land administration issues paper—World Bank Urban Upgrading project: Hai Phong and Ho Chi Minh City. Ho Chi Minh City: Australian Agency for International Development.

Gold, Thomas B., and Victoria Bonnell. 2002. Introduction. In *New Entrepreneurs of Europe and Asia: Patterns of Business Development in Russia, Eastern Europe and China*, ed. T. B. Gold and V. Bonnell. Armonk, N.Y.: M. E. Sharpe.

Goldhaber, Dale. 2000. *Theories of Human Development: Integrative Perspectives*. Mountain View: Mayfield Publishing.

Goodman, Allen C., and Masahiro Kawai. 1984. Functional form and rental housing market analysis. *Urban Studies* 21: 367–76.

Granovetter, Mark. 1983. The strength of weak ties: A network theory revisited. *Sociological Theory* 1: 201–33.

———. 1985. Economic action and social structure: The problem of embeddedness. *American Journal of Sociology* 91 (11): 481–510.

———. 2002. A theoretical agenda for economic sociology. In *The New Economic Sociology: Developments in an Emerging Field*, ed. M. F. Guillen, C. Randall, P. England and M. Meyer. New York: Russell Sage Foundation.

———. 2005. The impact of social structure in economic outcomes. *Journal of Economic Perspectives* 19 (1): 33–50.

Granovetter, Mark, Valery Yakubovich, and Patrick McGuire. 2005. Electric charges: The social construction of rate systems. *Theory and Society* 34 (5–6): 579–612.

Greif, Avner. 2006. *Institutions and the Path to the Modern Economy*. New York: Cambridge University Press.

———. 2005. Foreword: Institutions, Markets, and Games. In *The Economic Sociology of Capitalism*, ed. V. Nee and R. Swedberg. Princeton, N.J.: Princeton University Press.

Hall, Peter A., and David Soskice. 2001. *Varieties of Capitalism*. New York: Oxford University Press.

Harvey, David. 1989. From managerialism to entrepreneurialism: The transformation in urban governance in late capitalism. *Geografiska Annaler, Series B: Human Geography* 71 (1): 3–17.

HCMC Statistical Yearbook. 1997. *Ho Chi Minh City Statistical Yearbook.* Hanoi: Statistical Publishing House.

————. 2000. *Ho Chi Minh City Statistical Yearbook.* Hanoi: Statistical Publishing House.

Henrich, Joseph, Robert Boyd, Samuel Bowles, Colin Camerer, Ernst Fehr, and Herbert Gintis, eds. 2004. *Foundations of Human Sociality: Economic Experiments and Ethnographic Evidence from Fifteen Small-Scale Societies.* New York: Oxford University Press.

Heritage Foundation. 2004. *Index of Economic Freedom.* Washington, D.C.: Heritage Foundation and the Wall Street Journal.

Ho, Peter. 2005. *Institutions in Transition: Land Ownership, Property Rights and Social Conflict in China.* New York: Oxford University Press.

Hong, Nguyen. 2000. Housing planners think big, but financial reality keeps dawning. *Vietnam Investment Review,* January 31.

Hsing, You-tien. 1998. *Making Capitalism in China: the Taiwan Connection.* New York: Oxford University Press.

Human Rights Watch. 1997. Rural unrest in Vietnam. Human Rights Watch Report..

Ibbotson, Roger G., Laurence B. Siegel, and Kathryn S. Love. 1985. World Wealth: Market Values and Returns. *Journal of Portfolio Management* 12 (1): 4–23.

IMF. 2000. Focus on transition economies. In *IMF World Economic Outlook.* Washington, D.C.: International Monetary Fund.

JBIC. 1999. *Urban Development and Housing Sector in Viet Nam.* JBIC Research Paper no. 3. Tokyo: Japan Bank for International Cooperation.

Jimenez, Emmanuel. 1984. Tenure security and urban squatting. *Review of Economics and Statistics* 66 (4): 556–67.

Jones Lang LaSalle. 2006. Real Estate Transparency Index. Jones Lang LaSalle.

Kim, A. M. 2004. A market without the "right" property rights: Ho Chi Minh City, Vietnam's newly-emerged private real estate market. *Economics of Transition* 12 (2): 275–305.

————. 2007. North versus south: The impact of social norms in the market pricing of private property rights in Vietnam. *World Development* 35 (12): 2079–95.

Krueckeberg, Donald A. 2004. The Lessons of John Locke or Hernando de Soto: What if your Dreams Come True? *Housing Policy Debate* 15 (1): 1–24.

Lave, Jean, and Etienne Wenger. 1991. *Situated Learning: Legitimate Peripheral Participation.* Learning in Doing: Social, Cognitive, and Computational Perspectives. New York: Cambridge University Press.

Leaf, Michael. 1994. Legal authority in an extralegal setting: The case of land rights in Jakarta, Indonesia. *Journal of Planning Education and Research* 14: 12–18.

Leaf, Michael, and Nguyen Quang Vinh. 1996. City life in the village of ghosts: The development of popular housing in Ho Chi Minh City, Vietnam. *Habitat International* 20 (2): 175–90.

Li, Lianjiang, and Kevin J. O'Brien. 1996. Villagers and popular resistance in contemporary China. *Modern China* 22 (1): 28–61.

Li, Ling Hin. 1999. *Urban Land Reform in China.* New York: St. Martin's Press.

Lo, Vai Io, and Xiaowen Tian. 2002. Property Rights, Productivity Gains, and Economic Growth: The Chinese Experience. *Post-Communist Economies* 14 (2): 245–58.

Loewenstein, George. 1999. Experimental economics from the vantage-point of behavioural economics. *The Economic Journal* 109 (February): F25–F34.

Lopinski, R. 2005. The legal protection of dwelling under construction: Purchasers in Poland and in the chosen EU countries. *Zeszyt Hipoteczny* 19: 48–62.

Luan, Trinh Duy, Nguyen Quang Vinh, Brahm Wiesman, and Michael Leaf. 2000. Part II: Urban housing. In *Socioeconomic Renovation in Viet Nam: The Origin, Evolution, and Impact of Doi Moi,* ed. P. Boothroyd and P. X. Nam. Ottowa: IDRC.

Mantzavinos, Chrysostomos. 2001. *Individuals, Institutions, and Markets.* Cambridge: Cambridge University Press.

Mantzavinos, C., Douglass C. North, and Syed Shariq. 2004. Learning, Institutions, and Economic Performance. *Perspectives on Politics* 2 (1): 75–84.

McDermott, Gerald A. 2002. The embedded politics of entrepreneurship and network reconstructing in East-Central Europe. In *The New Entrepreneurs of Europe and Asia: Patterns of Business Development in Russia, Eastern Europe and China,* ed. V. E. Bonnell and T. B. Gold. Armonk, N.Y.: M. E. Sharpe.

Mekong Capital. 2007. *Reasons for Vietnam's Strong GDP Growth Rates.* Mekong Capital 2007 http://www.mekongcapital.com. [Accessed September 7 2007].

Moise, Edwin E. 1983. *Land Reform in China and North Vietnam.* Chapel Hill: University of North Carolina Press.

Mullainathan, Sendhil. 2007. Development economics through the lens of psychology. In *Behavioral Economics and its Applications,* ed. P. Diamond and H. Vartiainen. Princeton, N.J.: Princeton University Press.

Nee, Victor. 1989. A theory of market transition: From redistribution to markets in state socialism. *American Sociological Review* 54 (5): 663–81.

Nee, Victor. 1996. The emergence of a market society: Changing mechanisms of stratification in China. *American Journal of Sociology* 101 (4): 908–49.

Nee, Victor, and Richard Swedberg, eds. 2007. *On Capitalism*. Palo Alto, Calif.: Stanford University Press.

Nelson, Richard R. 2002. Bringing institutions into evolutionary growth theory. *Journal of Evolutionary Economics* 12: 17–28.

North, Douglass. 1991. Institutions. *Journal of Economic Perspectives* 5: 97–112.

———. 2005. *Understanding the Process of Economic Change*. Princeton, N.J.: Princeton University Press.

Oi, Jean C. 1995. The role of the local state in China's transitional economy. *China Quarterly* 144: 1132–49.

Pamuk, Ayse. 1996. Convergence trends in formal and informal housing markets: The case of Turkey. *Journal of Planning Education and Research* 16: 103–13.

Pei, Minxin. 2006. *China's Trapped Transition: The Limits of Developmental Autocracy*. Cambridge, Mass.: Harvard University Press.

Perkins, Dwight H. 2001. Industrial and financial policy in China and Vietnam. In *Rethinking the East Asia Miracle*, ed. J. Stiglitz and S. Yusuf. Washington, D.C.: World Bank.

Perkins, Dwight, Joseph Stern, Ji-Hong Kim, and Jung-Ho Kim. 1995. *Industrialization and the State: Korea's Heavy and Chemical Industry Drive*. Cambridge, Mass.: Harvard University Press.

Pingali, Prabhu L., and Vo-Tong Xuan. 1992. Vietnam: Decollectivization and rice productivity growth. *Economic Development and Cultural Change* 40 (1): 697–718.

Pipes, Richard. 1996. Human Nature and the Fall of Communism. *Academy of Arts and Sciences Bulletin* 54 (January): 38–52.

PMR Ltd. 2004. Residential construction in January 2004. *Polish Construction Review*, March, 5.

Pomeranz, Kenneth. 2001. *The Great Divergence: China, Europe, and the Making of the Modern World Economy*. Princeton, N.J.: Princeton University Press.

Posner, Richard A. and Eric B. Rasmusen. 1999. Creating and Enforcing Norms, with Special Reference to Sanctions. *International Review of Law and Economics* 19: 369–82.

Quynh, Vo Hong. 2000a. Article on the Hiep Phuc Industrial Zone. *Tuoi Tre*, July 18, 5.

———. 2000b. Final decision on complaints about "An Lac" supermarket to be announced in October. *Tuio Tre*, September 22, 14.

———. 2000c. State General Inspector Ta Huu Thanh: Resolving complaints must be in accordance with both feeling and reason/sensibility *Tuoi Tre*, September 23, 3.

———. 2000d. We ask for justice. *Tuoi Tre*, September 26, 13.

REAS Konsulting. 2002. *Warsaw Residential Market Report 2002/2003*. Warsaw: REAS.

Regulski, Jerzy. 2003. *Local Government Reform in Poland: An Insider's Story*. Local Government and Public Service Reform Initiative. Budapest: Open Society Institute.

Rodrik, Dani, Arvind Subramanian, and Francesco Trebbi. 2004. Institutions Rule: The Primacy of Institutions Over Geography and Integration in Economic Development. *Journal of Economic Growth* 9: 131–65.

Rodrik, Dani, and Romain Wacziarg. 2005. Do Democratic Transition Produce Bad Economic Outcomes. *American Economic Review, Papers and Proceedings* 95 (2): 50–55.

Rogers, E. M. 1983. *Diffusion of Innovations*. 3rd ed. New York: Free Press.

Rogoff, Barbara. 1990. *Apprenticeship in Thinking: Cognitive development in social context*. New York: Oxford University Press.

Roland, Gerard. 2000. *Transition and Economics: Politics, Markets, and Firms*. Cambridge, Mass.: MIT Press.

Rosen, Sherwin. 1974. Hedonic prices and implicit markets: Product differentiation in pure competition. *Journal of Political Economy* 82 (1): 34–55.

Sabel, Charles. 1994. Learning-by-Monitoring: the Institutions of Economic Development. In *Handbook of Economic Sociology*, eds. N.M. Smelser and R. Swedberg. Princeton, N.J.: Princeton University Press.

Sachs, Jeffrey D.. 1995. Postcommunist parties and the politics of entitlements. *Transitions* 6 (3): 1–4.

———. 1996. The Transition at Mid Decade. *American Economic Review* 86 (2): 128–33.

Saxenian, Anna Lee. 1996. *Regional Advantage*. Cambridge, Mass.: Harvard University Press.

Scharfstein, David S., and Jeremy C. Stein. 1990. Herd behavior and investment. *American Economic Review* 80 (3): 465–79.

Silbey, Susan S., and Patricia Ewick. 2003. Narrating social structure: Stories of resistance to legal authority. *American Journal of Sociology* 108 (6): 1328–72.

Skinner, B. F. 1953. *Science and Human Behavior*. New York: Free Press.

Stark, David. 1996. Recombinant property in East European capitalism. *American Journal of Sociology* 101 (4): 993–1027.

———. 2001. Ambiguous assets for uncertain environments: Heterarchy in postsocialist firms. In *The Twenty-First-Century Firm: Changing Economic Organization in International Perspective*, ed. P. DiMaggio. Princeton: Princeton University Press.

Stark, David, and Laszlo Bruszt. 2001. One way or multiple paths: For a comparative sociology of East European capitalism. *American Journal of Sociology* 106 (4): 1129–37.

Stiglitz, Joseph E. 1996. Some lessons From the East Asian miracle. *World Bank Research Observer* 11 (2): 151–77.

Svejnar, Jan. 1996. Enterprises and Workers in the Transition: Econometric Evidence. *The American Economic Review* 86 (2): 123–27.

Swedberg, Richard. 2005. The Economic Sociology of Capitalism: An introduction and agenda. In *The economic sociology of capitalism*, ed. V. Nee and R. Swedberg. Princeton, N.J.: Princeton University Press.

Szafarz, Piotr. 2003. Draft of the new zoning law: Act for equals and more equals. *Eurobuild Poland*, 34–35.

Tanner, Murray Scot. 2005. Chinese government responses to rising social unrest. Congressional Testimony before US–China Economic and Security Review Commission, U.S. Congress, Washington, D.C.

Trung, Xuan. 2000. Three cross-sector governmental delegates worked in Ha Tay, Dong Nai, HCM City: listens to complaints about the Anlac supermarket project. *Tuoi Tre*, September 26, 3.

Turley, William S., and Brantly Womack. 1998. Asian socialism's open doors: Guangzhou and Ho Chi Minh City. *China Journal* 40: 95–119.

Tversky, Amos, and Daniel Kahneman. 1974. Judgment under uncertainty: Heuristics and biases *Science* 185 (4157): 1124–31.

———. 1979. Prospect theory: An analysis of decision under risk. *Econometrica* 47: 263–91.

———. 1981. The framing of decision and the psychology of choice. *Science* 211: 453–58.

UNDP. 1995. Urban sector strategy study report. United Nations Development Program, Hanoi.

UNECE. 1997. *Human Settlements Trends in Central and Eastern Europe*. Geneva: United Nations Economic Commission for Europe.

Vietnam Chamber of Commerce and Industry. 2007. Access to land: Issues faced by private sector. In *Business Issues Bulletin*. Hanoi: Business Information Center, Vietnam Chamber of Commerce and Industry.

Vietnam Investment Review. 1998. Bright lights still shine in the big city. *Vietnam Investment Review*, September 14.

Vietnam Land Law 1993. Hanoi: National Political Publisher, August 1993.

Vietnam Land Law 2003. No.13/2003/QH11.

Vygotsky, Lev S. 1978. *Mind in Society: The development of higher psychological processes*. Cambridge, Mass.: Harvard University Press.

Wade, Robert. 2004. *Governing the Market: Economic theory and the role of government in East Asian industrialization*. Princeton, N.J.: Princeton University Press.

Watt, J. G., and S. A. van den Berg. 1978. Time series analysis of alternative media effects theories. In *Communication Yearbook 2*, ed. R. D. Ruben. New Brunswick, N.J.: Transaction Books.

Whitford, Josh. 2002. Pragmatism and the untenable dualism of means and ends: why rational choice theory does not deserve paradigmatic privilege. *Theory and Society* 31: 325–63.

Wiegersma, Nancy. 1988. *Vietnam—peasant land, peasant revolution: Patriarchy and collectivity in the rural economy.* New York: St. Martin's Press.

Williamson, Oliver. 1996. *Mechanisms of Governance.* Oxford: Oxford University Press.

Woodruff, Chirstopher, and John McMillan. 1999. Dispute prevention without courts in Vietnam. *Journal of Law, Economics, and Organization* 15 (3): 637–58.

————. 2002. The central role of entrepreneurs in transition economies. *Journal of Economic Perspectives* 16 (3): 153–70.

Woodruff, Christopher. 2001. Review of de Soto's *The Mystery of Capital. Journal of Economic Literature* 39: 1215–23.

World Bank. 2007. Vietnam striving to become middle-income country, World Bank president says. World Bank Press Release, no. 2008/43/ EAP.

Wrong, Dennis Hume. 1995. *Power: Its Forms, Bases, and Uses.* New Brunswick, N.J.: Transaction Publishers.

Wu, Fulong. 2002. China's changing urban governance in the transition towards a more market-oriented economy. *Urban Studies* 39 (7): 1071–93.

Yu, Tony Y. 1997. Entrepreneurial state: The role of government in the economic development of the Asian newly industrializing economies. *Development Policy Review* 15 (1): 47–64.

Zald, Mayer N. 1996. Culture, ideology, and strategic framing. In *Comparative Perspectives on Social Movements: Political Opportunities, Mobilizing Structures, and Cultural Framings,* ed. D. McAdam, J. D. McCarthy, and M. N. Zald. New York: Cambridge University Press.

Zerubavel, Eviatar. 1997. *Social Mindscapes: An Invitation to Cognitive Sociology.* Cambridge, Mass.: Harvard University Press.

Zhu, Jieming. 1999. Local growth coalition: The context and implications of China's gradualist urban land reforms. *International Journal of Urban and Regional Research* 23 (3): 534–48.

————. 2002. Urban development under ambiguous property rights: A case of China's transition economy. *International Journal of Urban and Regional Research* 26 (1): 41–57.

————. 2004. Local developmental state and order in China's urban development during transition. *International Journal of Urban and Regional Research* 28 (2): 424–47.

Index

agency
  new paradigms relating to, 17, 113,
    116
  structure v., 10, 12, 13, 16, 27, 117,
    184
approvals. *See* permits and approvals
Asian countries, economic
    development in, 7–8, 20, 21, 49,
    101, 139
Asian currency crisis, 82–84, 95–96,
    108*n*3
associations
  Retired People's Association, 66
  Women's Association, 66
attention
  learning and changing relating
    to, 113–14, 175, 176, 180, 183
  social structure and, in
    Warsaw, 158–60, 175

Bandura, 18, 112, 113, 116, 125, 129*n*1,
    184
bank loans, financing projects
    with, 73, 98
behavioral finance. *See* economics
behavioral models, human, 13–14, 15,
    112, 117

Berger, 16
Binh Chanh district, 39, 42
Binh Hung ward, 70
BOLUC. *See* Building Ownership and
    Land Use Certificate
Bourdieu, 12, 13, 19
Building Ownership and Land Use
    Certificate (BOLUC), 40, 137, 141,
    144, 146, 165*n*2
  ownership certificates, 141, 144
  pink certificates, 137–38, 140, 141,
    144–45, 147
  red certificates, 141, 144
Burawoy, 13, 19, 20, 24, 100, 101, 163
bureaucracy
  Communist, 38
  in Vietnam, 138
case firms relating to, 50, 173

"capacity building," 11, 181
capitalism
  essentials of transition and, 162–65,
    176, 178
  and institutions, 20, 21, 32, 110
  and land, 22–23, 28
  market, 8
  Marxist model of, 13, 101